CREATING A CUSTOM FIT IN
AN OFF-THE-RACK GENRE WORLD

THE PROXIMAL INVESTIGATOR, THE CORPSE OF CONVENIENCE, AND THEIR FAMILY OF CIRCUMSTANCE IN CRIME FICTION

Jay Verney PhD

ZKB

Zen Kettle Books
BRISBANE

Zen Kettle Books
Contact (all enquiries): steaming@zenkettle.com
www.zenkettle.com

Book Cover Design ©Zen Kettle Design at zenkettle.com
Book Layout ©2013 BookDesignTemplates.com

Also available as an ebook

National Library of Australia Cataloguing-in-Publication Entry

Verney, Jay.

Creating A Custom Fit In An Off-The-Rack Genre World: The Proximal Investigator, The Corpse of Convenience, and Their Family of Circumstance in Genre Fiction.

Detective and mystery stories—History and criticism.

Dewey Number: A809.3872

ISBN 978-0-9873779-8-2

Dedicated to all the even more dedicated gumshoe researchers – you know who you are, comrades, and if you don't you have the skills to find out.

It takes three to tango in my world, Myfanwy, dear: the poor dead schlub inside the chalk outline, the cracking crowd of maybe babies who might just have put him there – and me, kiddo. Now put that gun down and pick up the phone. We need double decaf lattes with extra foam and we need them now. Myfanwy? Put down the gun. Myfanwy?

—from Frances M. Lazar, THE LONGEST NAP
(Unpublished manuscript, circa 1993)

Table of Contents

Introduction

Dear Reader,

A few years ago, perhaps due to lunacy or being in a delusional state, I decided to research a PhD in Creative Writing. I decided this even before I knew if I'd score any financial support to do it, or an office in which to cogitate and eat lunch. Mad as. After months (or maybe it was weeks, could have been minutes, who remembers?) of hopeful waiting and drinking tea (no, it was months and many hundreds of tea bags), my proposal was accepted, a mysterious group of people decided the government would send me a stipend in the form of scholarship money (rather than cabbages) every fortnight, and I was on my way.

The thesis took approximately three and a half years to complete and a lot of days and nights staring at my cats, who stared back, as cats do. For the record, may I say that they offered no assistance other than their constant, loving though indifferent presence, and demands for steak tartare (*sans* accessories) and grated cheese.

The trauma of completing a PhD should not be underestimated, and for any of you reading who may be contemplating such a move, remember this: do it for reasons that will sustain you through the several years of your candidature, loving cats and partners notwithstanding.

Naturally, you have to work out the reasons all by yourself. Here are some worthy suggestions to get you started: (a) you really want to be called Doctor by the crummy kids who bullied you in primary school (even though many of them are dead now: see zombie apocalypse below); (b) you may never make this much money again out of writing, should you manage to snag a scholarship; (c) walking around campus knowing you'll have an office to hide in when the zombie apocalypse strikes unexpectedly will be (temporarily at least) reassuring (and you can laugh at the limbless, bloody zombies from your sixth floor window); (d) you're pretty much useless or only passable at other occupations, and writing, hey, how hard can it be, dude – forget that last bit. Finally, (e) you need somewhere, anywhere to go in the daytime when the rest of your family is trooping off to their gainful employment and you're left with the breakfast bacon rind and two cats impersonating Lee Van Cleef's narrow-eyed stare. You're welcome to use any of these handily alphabetised motivations. Of course, they do not apply to me in any way.

The reason I'm publishing this essay is because I spent so much time and effort researching and writing it, and these days it languishes in the electronic records system of the library of the august institution from which I received my just desserts (cheesecake, if you must know) and a Dean's Award (Dean is a lovely fellow, I must say). Even though enrolled students can access the records should they choose, and a somewhat surprising (to me) number have done so, very few others can. I, for instance, cannot, not any more, since I'm no longer a student. Isn't life funny like that? You write something and it disappears and furthermore, you can't even look upon its beauty as it reclines in its splendid electronic university raiment.

Anyway, dear reader, I rescued my novel, *Summon Up The Blood*, which is the other half of the thesis (it was called "Thicker Than Water" originally, as you'll learn when you read on, as I'm sure you will after this sales pitch), from its shackles in the dimly lit halls of academe (actually, they're quite bright, but 'dimly-lit' has a certain *je ne sais quoi* about it, don't you think?). It's available as a paperback and an ebook, and I'm doing the same for this essay. Here at the Two

Cat Cafe we say share the research, share the love, share the bacon rind and grated cheese, and any spare cabbages you may possess.

Without further delay, please enjoy this educational and perhaps, dare one hope, even entertaining reading experience. The Abstract which follows relates to the entire thesis, but now you know that the novel bit is elsewhere (on Amazon actually) reclining in its very own (and quite adorable) published raiment and also waiting for your beautiful eyes to fall upon it.

Yours in serious silliness
Jay Verney (Cat Wrangler and Purveyor of Fine Mince)

Abstract

This thesis consists of two components: a creative work, "Thicker Than Water," and a critical essay, "Creating a Custom Fit in an Off-the-Rack (Genre) World." [Note: "Thicker Than Water" became the published novel, *Summon Up The Blood*, an altogether more thrilling title if you ask me].

"Thicker Than Water" is a crime novel that may be positioned in the sub-genre of the thriller, while also incorporating some elements of the detective, mystery, and organised crime sub-genres. It involves an Olympic gold medallist and art gallery owner, Livia Galvin, in murders, kidnapping, and a hunt for stolen art treasures. The narrative begins with scenes in Bogota, Beijing, and the Strait of Magellan, but is set largely in River City (a fictionalised version of Brisbane, Queensland) immediately following the 2008 Beijing Olympics. After being attacked by two would-be assassins in Beijing, Livia returns to River City to discover that her godmother and close Galvin family friend and business colleague, Minnie Babitsky, has apparently been murdered. Livia is drawn into the quest to find Minnie's killer, beginning a journey of self-discovery and revelations about her family and their criminal connections. The novel is an example of the evolutionary and hybrid nature of the crime genre, and of genres in general, issues which I discuss in the critical essay in relation to investigator-based murder fiction.

In murder fiction, three kinds of characters are usually present: the murder victims, the investigators, and the suspects. It is possible to position these characters along a creative continuum moving from the relatively formulaic to the relatively unique, incorporating two-dimensional, stock characters and more fully-realised human beings. The essay, "Creating a Custom Fit in an Off-the-Rack (Genre) World," explores some of the ways in which such characters function individually and in relation to each other to effect a 'same but different' reading experience, how they contribute to creating a custom fit in the notionally off-the-rack world of genre fiction. One of the questions the essay asks, therefore, is how do these characters operate in murder fiction to achieve a sense of difference in their roles even as they abide by established conventions and demonstrate many traits and behaviours similar to other investigators, victims, and suspects? In short, how do they flout convention while following it? How do they contribute to the genre's evolution and development?

In the essay, I have coined specific terms for each of the character roles of investigator and murder victim: the proximal investigator and the corpse of convenience, respectively; and a collective term for the suspects, remembering that, initially, everyone is suspect: the family of circumstance. The idea of using generic terms such as these for a diverse range of investigators, victims, and suspects may at first seem to defeat the purpose of emphasising their potential uniqueness. But when seen as part of a continuum or spectrum, I suggest that such terms of classification help to highlight the traits that differentiate these characters from each other. They serve as a means by which both author and reader can remind themselves and be reminded of the increasingly diverse range of characters to be found in contemporary crime fiction, regardless of their 'special' skills as crime investigators. Further, when applied to specific texts, they may offer a useful means of considering the sub-genres which murder fiction encompasses from both diachronic and synchronic viewpoints.

CHAPTER ONE

Creating a Custom Fit: G is for Genre and C is for Crime

INTRODUCTION

The central question of this essay reframes its title to reflect the challenge of creating a 'same but different' reading experience in genre fiction: how does an author create a text that is a custom fit, that is, different from the others in its genre or sub-genre, but not so very different that it appears less than recognisable, or alien, in a popular form like crime fiction, where endless repetition and adherence to a limited range of conventions and techniques are the apparent norms? In this essay, I respond to the question of how to create a custom-fit text by focusing on character roles and characterisation strategies as they appear in selected texts in the sub-genres that I describe as investigator-based murder novels. These are novels in which the principal crime is murder, and a character identifiable as an investigator of some kind (even an accidental one) seeks, or is persuaded, to solve the crime.

These sub-genres, which include the clue-puzzle (the Jane Marple novels are representative of this sub-genre), the private detective (Sherlock Holmes), the hard-boiled private eye (Sam Spade, V. I. Warshawski), the police procedural (Inspector Kurt

Wallander), the forensic procedural (Kay Scarpetta), and the amateur sleuth (Kate Fansler) forms, also serve to illustrate the hybrid and evolutionary nature of crime fiction, and of genres in general. Hybridisation, defined as either the combination of at least two genres to form a new genre or sub-genre, or the integration of elements from two or more genres within a text (Duff xiv), is the context in which "Thicker Than Water" was written. Crime fiction is demonstrably a hybrid genre, consisting of a range of sub-genres that have evolved over the better part of the last 200 years. Many of these sub-genres, or elements of them, such as the forensic and police procedurals, may be seen in embryonic form in stories by Sir Arthur Conan Doyle featuring Holmes, and in novels such as Wilkie Collins's The Moonstone. The novel I wrote as part of this thesis is, itself, a hybrid text, employing, for example, structural, plotting, and characterisation conventions both of traditional mystery and detective fiction. In addition, it borrows from the thriller and organised crime family sub-genres, and contains elements of the kind of crime novels Patricia Highsmith excelled at in her Ripley stories, where arguably amoral characters operate outside the world of policing and 'law-abiding' society even as they function with relatively apparent ease within it.

Along with this mix of sub-genres, the dominant characterisation convention in "Thicker Than Water" is the presence of an investigator, Livia Galvin. My decision to foreground character-related issues arose partly from the novel's genesis in this single character, and partly from my research into crime fiction and, more specifically, contemporary crime fiction featuring investigators. Although my approach to developing a story begins, as it does for many authors, with character, it was also clear to me from my reading of a range of crime texts that the ways in which the protagonists in these texts are depicted are of primary relevance to the levels of suspense and interest that the narrative has the capacity to develop, apart from the complexities of the plot. Characterisation matters a great deal in contemporary crime series. Further, these levels of interest and suspense are not only directed towards the service of crime solving in that the aim, in many of these texts, is to present these characters as three-dimensional individuals whose lives incorporate detection together with other elements – familial, social, political, economic, geographic. Frequently, these other parts of their lives draw the characters into investigations. The investigations, in turn, inform and affect the other aspects of their lives. Such texts are successfully marketed from this perspective: the cover blurb on Sara Paretsky's Fire Sale begins, "A favour to an old friend means a return to the streets of South Chicago for V. I. Warshawski." The novels are clearly promoted as featuring a flesh and blood protagonist/investigator: "V. I. Warshawski is a private eye who's short of clients" (Indemnity Only).(Note 1: In the editions that I own (Hodder and Stoughton, Hamish Hamilton, Penguin), each novel in the Warshawski series promotes Warshawski as the major drawcard, the reason to buy, and this is the rule rather than the exception for series-based characters. The Warshawski novels offer a variety of promotional techniques, including simple one-liners: "A V. I. Warshawksi novel" (Fire Sale); a line from a Guardian newspaper review: "Thank heavens for V. I. Warshawski" (Bitter Medicine); a tie-in to the film adaptation: "As seen in the film V. I. Warshawski starring Kathleen Turner" (Deadlock); and as part of the title: V. I. for Short (a collection of short stories). The investigators are the ones who are burdened with contributing most tellingly to the creation of custom-fit texts, through the expression of their own individuality and through the exposition of their relationships with, and attitudes towards other characters, especially the suspects and the victims.

It is primarily for these reasons that I focus on character roles and characterisation strategies in this essay, in which I argue for three alternative perspectives: the proximal investigator, the corpse of convenience, and the family of circumstance, from which one might consider the protagonists, the victims, and the suspects, respectively. My aim is to consider how these characters participate in particular texts to help them achieve, simultaneously, their intertwined goals of sameness and difference. I discuss each of these alternatives below, before turning to a consideration of genre, genre analogies, and crime fiction, in order to contextualise my argument and the position of investigator-based murder novels, both in series and one-off forms.

THE PROXIMAL INVESTIGATOR

The protagonists or investigators in murder novels are known variously as amateurs, private eyes, police detectives, forensic pathologists, as sleuths of one sort or another. I apply the term 'proximal investigator' to replace the range of detecting types and the collective description and perception of them as heroic figures, where proximal refers to the investigator's nearness to, closeness or adjacency with the situation surrounding the criminal activity. My aim is to set aside traditional generic labels and use a more neutral descriptor relatively free of particular expectations. The question then arises as to how the proximal investigator's position relative to specific sites of proximity affects their role as protagonist, investigator, and crime fighting hero. These sites of proximity include other characters, landscapes, and ideas: political, social, racial, spiritual, ethical, philosophical, and so on. One of the implied messages in the investigator-based sub-genres, after all, is that only this particular character with their unique personality, possessing their specific range of skills, attributes, and connections, is capable of solving this mystery, this crime, at this time. At each outing, the proximal investigator undertakes a journey that resembles, to a greater or lesser degree, the hero's quest or journey, and this notion of heroism is another site of proximity. Isn't solving crimes, by its very nature, heroic, and don't we, as readers, enjoy assuming heroic roles with our protagonists?

It is possible to see the proximal investigator from a variety of heroic perspectives throughout the history of the genre. Holmes, for example, in the last decades of the British Empire, as Dennis Porter points out, is "the polished, chivalrous hero" who represents the "popular supersleuth who functioned as the chosen instrument for joining crime to its solution in the age of jingoism" (156). He embodies the Empire, and lives in a world in which crime can be contained and where stability is the norm. By contrast, although Raymond Chandler's "mean streets" private eye "is the hero, he is everything .... He must be the best man in his world, and a good enough man for any world" ("Simple" 237), his heroic status is based in an "updated version of a traditional warrior code," in which his life is one of "duty and renunciation in between bouts of loose living" (Porter 183). In a decentred, unstable world where corruption is the norm, and his own life is at constant risk, self-preservation may involve fighting the enemy at the enemy's level (163) and, in any case, Spade and Philip Marlowe are men of the people even in their solitary lives, neither supporters of institutional policing structures nor of criminals (169). Their heroism is based in a kind of ordinariness made extraordinary by their willingness to place themselves in harm's way to right a wrong or avenge a death. Their strength is not "as the strength of ten" because their hearts, like Sir Galahad's, are pure (Tennyson 48), but because they know how to handle themselves outside, and often well beneath, the Marquis of Queensbury's rules of ethical fighting, and they are willing to do so. The hard-boiled detective, as John Cawelti (42) and Carl Malmgren (103) note, can be seen as a kind of archetypal adventure hero on a quest to right wrongs and rescue society from itself.

The proximal investigator in contemporary murder novels treads a sometimes delicate and fine line between moral or ethical absolutes and their relative counterparts, but always with the aim of protecting the innocent and punishing the guilty in pursuit of the quest. The hero's journey has been seen by Vladimir Propp, Carl Jung, Joseph Campbell, and Christopher Vogler, among many others, as existing in a variety of forms: in the myths, folk tales, and stories of societies around the world and throughout recorded history. (Note 2: In The Writer's Journey: Mythic Structure for Storytellers and Screenwriters, Christopher Vogler offers an updated version of Joseph Campbell's hero's journey, described in The Hero with a Thousand Faces. Some, or all of these elements may be found in investigator-based murder novels, and I found on re-reading that my novel, "Thicker Than Water," reflects this journey, too. Vogler's stages of the hero's journey are: 1. Ordinary World. 2. Call to Adventure. 3. Refusal of the Call. 4. Meeting with the Mentor. 5. Crossing the First Threshold. 6. Tests, Allies, Enemies. 7. Approach to the Inmost Cave. 8. Ordeal. 9. Reward (Seizing the Sword). 10.

The Road Back. 11. Resurrection. 12. Return with the Elixir (14)). In contemporary crime fiction, self-deprecation and humour are often used in preference to, but also frequently along with fighting prowess and physical resilience, to depict the proximal investigator as almost an apologetic hero, highly motivated to right wrongs and re-establish order and safety, willing to use physical force or defensive techniques when required, but averse to accolades, and desirous of completing the job, often so that they can spend more time with friends and/or family, and simply return to their 'ordinary' worlds.

One version of this archetypal story that is relevant to some representations of the contemporary proximal investigator is concerned with a person, who is earmarked to become the hero, living a relatively ordinary life. They conduct their usual domestic (the amateur) or workplace (the private eye, the police inspector) routines (Smilla Jaspersen fortifying her solitude and maintaining her emotional distance from her father; Warshawski background-checking insurance claimants; Wallander tidying up the loose ends of minor crimes by taking statements and re-interviewing suspects). They are called upon (sometimes reluctantly, particularly with accidental or amateur sleuths) to save the day when some kind of tragic, life-changing incident occurs (in the case of the murder novel, the event is homicide) somewhere nearby. In the murder novel, when society's equilibrium is disturbed and a level of chaos emerges, it is the proximal investigator's role to enter this chaotic sphere, investigate the crime and restore equilibrium, albeit in a new and altered form, since there can never be a return to the same state of order that existed prior to the crime. During this narrative journey, the proximal investigator is likely to encounter obstacles, threats, enemies, allies, mentors, and shapeshifters, before solving the crime. The blending of these elements of action, interaction, investigation, and reflection, and the nature of the journey itself as purposeful, readily lend themselves to the hero's quest model. But it is also the case that we may take this collective label of hero not so much for granted but as a given, in the sense that with these protagonists, however ordinary or extraordinary they may appear, their heroism goes without saying. It is acknowledged and visible, on display from the moment one recognises the investigator's name promoting the latest title in a series, and from the moment the investigator engages with the narrative. Therefore, in this essay, I focus on the concept of the proximal investigator as a character who engages with particular sites of proximity in the course of an investigative journey of reconstruction and progressive exposition, and whose major narrative goal is the solving of a crime. These sites of proximity may be many or few, and part of the success of a 'same but different' reading experience is tied to a balance of quantity and depth of development, and to the timely and appropriate inclusion of such sites in a given narrative.

THE CORPSE OF CONVENIENCE

An essential site of proximity in investigator-based murder novels is that of death, in the form of the crime or murder scene and, by extension, the victim, referred to in this essay as the 'corpse of convenience.' I begin with the assertion that every homicide victim in murder texts is present for the convenience of the plot and, therefore, for the investigator and, further, that there are types and degrees of convenience to be considered. Towards one end of a continuum of emotional involvement or reaction, where depth of grief is demonstrably minimal, we find the corpse of greatest convenience. The victim's death is entirely expeditious for the plot, involving little or no grief for the surviving characters. This is the case in the clue-puzzle sub-genre, where the exposition and explanation of the ingenious murder plot is of most importance, and the victim is frequently depicted as unlikeable, or even loathsome (Colonel Protheroe in Agatha Christie's The Murder at the Vicarage, for example), in order to focus attention on questions of who, and how, and the mechanics of the mystery. Towards the other end of this continuum, the victim is depicted lovingly and represents a catastrophic loss for the survivors; the degree of expedience is all but invisible (the little boy, Isaiah, in Peter Høeg's Miss Smilla's Feeling for Snow). The narrative momentum and primary focus here, initially at least, relates to why the victim was murdered, ahead of who committed the crime, and how. The investigative reaction is driven more by grief and pain than by curiosity and intellectual challenge.

There are many other focal points between total expedience and total devastation where elements of each are combined to a greater or lesser degree. One may argue that the sub-genres representing individual agency, involving amateurs in particular, but also some private eyes – many of whom garner cases on the basis of personal connections (Paretsky's novels, for instance) – tend to be associated with a continuum of emotional involvement that generates levels of grief. In the sub-genres involving institutional investigation, or collective agency, such as the police procedural, we may argue that, while sympathetic, or even empathic grief may be present, the overriding aspect of emotional involvement can be best expressed as a level of performance satisfaction. While there should be no difference, theoretically, in the depth of job satisfaction derived from capturing and punishing the murderer of a drug dealer, for instance, compared to the murderers of an elderly couple (as in Henning

Mankell's Faceless Killers), human nature dictates otherwise. The commitment of a police team to solving a crime from which high levels of work satisfaction may be derived, appears to be proportionate to the perceived 'innocence' of the victims, though this 'innocence' may be tested as the investigation continues. Indeed, there is room for deriving an even better custom fit from a corpse of convenience who won't be pigeon-holed or pushed towards either end of the continuum of emotional involvement because this facilitates the further and more personal engagement of the proximal investigator with death itself.

The proximal investigators in murder novels must face death, both as observers of criminal acts that have led to homicide, and sometimes as potential victims themselves. The reader faces death vicariously through the eyes of the protagonist, and as a witness to the narrative of mortality. Cawelti suggests that the detective story is a kind of filter that acts to diffuse the horrors of murder and other outrageous crimes via the detachment of the investigator, and the form's "mediating structure" (131). As readers, we can feel the protection of this figure as we negotiate a landscape of fear, albeit with its underlying promise of simultaneous thrills and voyeuristic fulfilment, but it is a landscape that also offers comfort, the comfort of convention and the expectation of resolution, the dissipation of the fear along with its afterglow of satisfaction. As a writer, I engage with Margaret Atwood's suggestion that all writing, and certainly all writing of the narrative kind, "is motivated, deep down, by a fear of and a fascination with mortality – by a desire to make the risky trip to the Underworld, and to bring something or someone back from the dead" (140). We fear death and we want to be remembered after death, somehow. Atwood argues that writing, alone of all the creative arts, gives us and gives the dead, a voice, a kind of immortality and permanence: "what is written down is a score for voice" (142), and this voice tells a story. In the case of murder texts, the narrative, the 'score for voice,' is the reconstruction of the crime via the investigation, where the event of the crime itself marks the beginning of a state of disequilibrium from which the characters only emerge once the murderer is found and brought to justice. In this essay, I look at how representations of death contribute to creating the custom fit murder novel through the interplay of disparate relationships forged among major and minor characters, anchored by the connections between the proximal investigator and the corpse (or corpses) of convenience. This figure may act as a mere plot point, as the most convenient body of all, as a loved one whose loss is nothing short of an irreducible tragedy, or as a contributor to vocational nirvana in pursuit of the custom fit. He or she, as the essential site of proximity, always remains a special member of at least one family, the family of circumstance; the corpse of convenience is the character that draws this family together.

The Family of Circumstance

A family can be "any group of people connected by blood or other relationship" (New 1: 914). In other words, families are groups of people who are biologically related, or who are related through marriage, or groups who share something in common. The term family may also be employed in a metaphorical sense to denote the kinds of relationships and dynamics of a given group of people as being family-like or incorporating a family's attributes. For the purposes of my argument in this essay, I describe the entire cast of characters that appears in any investigator-based murder novel as a 'family of circumstance,' where the term family assumes both literal and meta-phorical significance. I take the position that the proximal investigator and the corpse of convenience assume special status within this group, and that the group collectively represents the suspects. Once the murder occurs, the corpse of convenience becomes a kind of honorary member of the group, the reason for its formation and its continuing togetherness at a particular time and place. The investigator has a special status, too, as the figure who is expected to restore equilibrium to the group – and, often, depending on the sub-genre, to society at large – by solving the crime (or crimes). All the surviving characters, including the proximal investigator, however unlikely, are regarded as suspects initially, following standard police procedure in homicide (and other) investigations. The proximal investigator will always, in theory at least, be a suspect – The Murder of Roger Ackroyd, and imitators of the combination character who is both unreliable narrator and murderer ensure that this is the case – even if they remain so only briefly. There can be no removal of this character from the family of circumstance when, in every novel, each of these families is brought together for particular reasons, just as families of circumstance develop in life.

The word family is used extensively in contemporary society to describe groups of individuals with special interests in common and may include, for example, members of trade unions fighting for workers' rights; members of gay, lesbian, transexual, transgender, and intersex groups concerned to establish equal rights and provide support for sexual minorities; and corporations whose public relations arms are at pains to stress the supportive environment in which their workers and potential workers operate. (Note 3: I have noted some examples when watching news reports or cultural events, and when surfing the Internet. For instance, during the Patrick's waterfront dispute with the Maritime Union of Australia, the then ACTU President, Jenny George, described the union movement as a family which would protect every one of its members from external threats; the Sister Sledge song, "We Are Family," is regarded as something of a gay anthem; and early in 2006, the then Coles-Myer corporation's recruitment web pages contained phrases such as, "Welcome to the K-Mart family"). Similarly, almost any group of characters portrayed in a television drama or comedy series (from Grey's Anatomy to Will and Grace, to The West Wing), has been described, or self-describes as a family at some point in the life of the series, regardless of biological or traditional definitions. The term, family, rather like genre, demonstrates both flexible and rigid boundaries. It may be engaged with both inclusively and exclusively, within and beyond workplaces, within and beyond domestic residences, within and beyond biological restrictions. All this encouraged my adoption of the term, family, in relation to the cast of characters in investigator-based murder fiction.

Unless one is reading or writing about organised crime families, it is seldom the case that the idea of the family springs to mind in the world of crime fiction and, in particular, the world of investigator-based murder novels. When it does, it is usually in relation to biological families, or groups perceived as existing in the traditional mould of a family unit, traumatised after one (or more) of their members is murdered. Even then, the notion of the family is rarely of primary concern. Yet, the family has been present in one form or another in crime fiction since Edgar Allan Poe created Chevalier Auguste Dupin and paired him with his faithful narrator. There are instances, throughout the development of the genre, of groups of characters that associate with the proximal investigator in ways suggestive of familial behaviours.

Conan Doyle established the dyad of Holmes and Dr Watson, partly in homage to Poe's earlier duo, and partly because Holmes needed a foil and storyteller, a loyal and trustworthy observer of his exploits. Marple is visited and surrounded by relatives, friends, and fellow villagers, the village itself performing the role of a very stable family group with its own mores and norms, so that the presence of deviance in the form of murder is even more acutely felt and shocking. Even Spade, hard-boiled loner, has a (problematic) relationship with fellow private eye and business partner, Miles Archer, whose murder in The Maltese Falcon Spade must investigate, not only because it's "bad business" to let a detective's killer get away with it, but also because, "When a man's partner is killed he's supposed to do something about it. It doesn't make any difference what you thought of him. He was your partner and you're supposed to do something about it" (213-14). This suggests tribal loyalty, identification with a particular social group and the protection, defence, and maintenance of the group against outside threats; it would not be out of place from a police officer in a police or forensic procedural novel. With slight variations, the sentiments apply equally to the relationships among members of criminal organisations.

Writing "Thicker Than Water" focused my attention on contemporary families in crime fiction and, initially, this focus was on depictions of characters in criminally connected family groups in novels and in film and television. Television series such as The Sopranos, which revolves around a New Jersey organised-crime family headed by Tony Soprano, have fulfilled the promise of Mario Puzo's highly influential novel, The Godfather, which was also adapted to film, in depicting organised crime from a fresh perspective. Promotional trailers for the first season of The Sopranos emphasise the character of Tony Soprano as mob boss, husband, father, and son but, by the second season, the catchphrase "Family. Redefined.," embraces and highlights other members of Tony's biological, crime, and extended families. Tony remains the pivotal character, a villainous hero figure on personal and professional quests, but there are also stronger spotlights on the interconnectedness of his relationships with members of both of his families, along with the complications associated with a succession of goomahs, or mistresses, in some ways another type of family group. His psychiatrist, Dr Jennifer Melfi, acts as a kind of de facto consigliere, or trusted adviser, a psychotherapeutic Tom Hagan, as it were. Tony's sessions with her are a means by which he attempts to understand and synthesise the different and too frequently conflicting aspects of his life (and her office, unbeknownst to her initially, provides the venue for Tony to meet a woman, one of Melfi's patients, who becomes Tony's mistress). Through her direct connection with Tony as his therapist, Melfi becomes an important member of both families, though she is neither biologically related nor criminally involved. Members of each group are unaware or barely aware of her existence, and her influence on their father and godfather. She becomes, in essence, a member of these combined families: an über-family which is, indeed, redefined.

Although "Thicker Than Water" is based in the activities of an organised crime family, my emphasis is on the character, Livia Galvin, as the proximal investigator of her family and friends, rather than on the Tony Soprano godfather figure of her Uncle Con Galvin. From Livia's perspective, I extend the notion of family beyond the biological, that is, beyond her immediate family of origin (her parent and sibling) and beyond her family of choice (Note 4:The family of choice is also known as the family of orientation: "a kinship group united not necessarily by blood but by such factors as common residence, shared experiences and backgrounds, mutual affection, and economic dependency" (Barker 54)). (her [ex]husband and son, together with friends such as Minnie Babitsky, Gordon Trembath, Grady Crabtree, and Ishmael Darrow), to encompass her family of circumstance, a group of people connected by their status as characters in the novel, all of them initially regarded as suspects, however briefly. In contemporary investigator-based murder novels, it is this family of circumstance that, in a broad sense, determines the nature of the custom fit text. Increasingly, proximal investigators are depicted as characters that lead lives apart from their investigative work, incorporating these various family groups as the narrative demands, and expanding the range of sites of proximity available for exploitation.

Any discussion of these three alternative perspectives on the investigator, the victim, and the suspects needs to take place in the context of a consideration of the genre of crime fiction. In the remainder of this chapter I discuss the nature of genres and the nature, specifically, of crime fiction as a popular genre. I argue that the family resemblance theory, proposed by Ludwig Wittgenstein and adapted by numerous theorists and critics as a genre analogy, is an ideal metaphor through which to view crime fiction and to demonstrate its hybrid, evolutionary nature. I present definitions of genre and of crime fiction to contextualise my overall aim: to illustrate the challenge of achieving the custom fit text by studying a range of contemporary investigator-based murder novels from the perspectives of proximal investigator, corpse of convenience, and family of circumstance. I continue here with genre, genre analogies, and crime fiction.

G IS FOR GENRE AND GENRE ANALOGIES

Definitions and discussions of genre and genre fiction – in particular, crime fiction – may be located along continuums of complexity beginning, for example, with the basic distinctions among prose, poetry, and drama (Gelder 42). But can genre as a concept, or the specifics of a particular genre, such as crime fiction, be clearly defined? This essay, which cannot be an extensive study of genre or genre theory as such, focusses on a particular historical genre, crime fiction, and is based in "observation[s] of literary reality" (Todorov, *The Fantastic* 13). It is contextually helpful, however, to offer a response to the question of genre as a concept, before moving on to the specifics of crime fiction. According to The New Shorter Oxford English Dictionary, genre means a kind or a type, especially a kind or class of novel, for example, characterised by "a particular form or purpose" (1:1076). In keeping with this, Ken Gelder describes a genre as "the type or species of fiction being written" (40). David Duff offers a "recurring type or category of text, as defined by structural, thematic, and/or functional criteria" (xiii). These relatively uncontentious definitions are useful as a starting point when responding to genre as a concept.

From the understanding of genres as entities that demonstrate hybridity, the concept of genre as a type or species, a recurring category of text, prompts a consideration of the observation of Russian Formalist, Yuri Tynyanov, that individual genres evolve through "dislocation" as new works appear which provoke and challenge the existing rules and conventions and are eventually incorporated into a particular genre's body of texts, thereby altering it. Every addition to a genre results in some change, even if this is radical or slight. Genres are, according to Tynyanov, evolutionary in nature, and therefore a "static definition of a genre, one which would cover all its manifestations, is impossible" (32). As Alastair Fowler succinctly argues, "definitions of genre can hardly be stated, before they are falsified" (42). Fowler is resistant to the idea of definitions as such, although, as I discuss below, he (along with David Fishelov and others) embraces the idea of Wittgenstein's family resemblance theory as one way to address this problem. Employing the concept of family resemblance as a genre analogy, Fowler argues that this approach facilitates an understanding of genres as having more to do with "identifying and communicating" rather than with "defining and classifying" (38), an open- rather than a closed-door approach to the nature of these entities. But resistance to definitions doesn't prevent them from being formulated, from notions of what a 'royal' or 'dominant' genre such as the novel constitutes, to the most specific rules within which, for example, a police procedural, a sub-genre of crime fiction, 'should' be written. Nor does it mean that such offerings are unwelcome or irrelevant. They are, rather, part both of the nature of genre as an overarching concept: a type or species of text, and of specific genres, such as crime fiction. They can contribute to forcing the door a little further open, and they can assist in engaging with analogies such as the family resemblance analogy as a means of characterising the diversity of a genre such as crime fiction and its evolutionary status.

The evolutionary nature of genre supports its position as a "socio-historical" entity (Todorov, Mikhail 80), that is, it is influenced by social and historical trends. An author's "generic concept," therefore, must be rooted in both diachronic and synchronic considerations, as they look back for models to imitate and exceed, and also at the wide range of works that are relevant now, contemporaneous with their own practice (Colie 30-31). A fuller definition of what constitutes a genre, in order to typologise the specific genre of crime fiction and its sub-genres, is offered by Fishelov: "a combination of prototypical, representative members, and a flexible set of constitutive rules that apply to some levels of literary texts, to some individual writers, usually to more than one literary period, and to more than one language and culture" (8). Fishelov characterises the prototypical members of a genre as the "hard core" members with a "high degree of resemblance" to each other (63). In applying this definition to crime fiction, part of the hard core would be the private eye or hard-boiled detective fiction popularised by Dashiell Hammett and Chandler in the 1920s and 1930s, and updated by authors like Peter Corris from the 1980s on.

In addition to this hard core of highly typical members, Fishelov argues for the inclusion of less typical works on the basis of shared traits that may be more obvious in some works than in others. To do this, he adopts Wittgenstein's family resemblance theory – also supported by Fowler, as mentioned above – to engage with the concept of genre by acting as an analogy, that is, the family represents a group of people who are related, and a genre consists of a group of texts that are regarded as its members (Fishelov 56). Wittgenstein's family resemblance theory does not require that all members of a family, or genre, share a single trait, even though they may have many traits in common, this also being the case with biological families. Or to put it another way, "representations of a genre," according to Fowler, "may then be regarded as making up a family whose septs and individual members are related in various ways, without necessarily having any single feature shared in common by all" (41). Further to Wittgenstein's theory, though, when discussing a study by Maurice Mandelbaum, Fishelov points out that, while Wittgenstein concentrated on promoting the "openness" of the idea of the family, he appeared to ignore the essential "stable" element that family members are related through common ancestry. This is the one trait, he argues, that is shared by all members of a biological family, and it may also be applied to genres (65).

The notion of common ancestry is supported by Fowler on the family resemblance analogy, where he asserts that generic resemblances are produced by literary tradition: "a sequence of influence and imitation and inherited codes connecting works in the genre. As kinship makes a family, so literary relations of this sort form a genre" (42). Poe, writing in the 1840s, and whose works I discuss in chapter two, is regarded by many as the originator of the modern detective story; he may be seen as one of the 'parents' of the genre of crime fiction. There are others, both earlier and later than Poe, who may be seen in a parental role, such as William Godwin, author of Caleb Williams (1794), the story of a young man falsely accused and hunted as a criminal, and Wilkie Collins, who wrote The Moonstone (1860), which features some of the earliest police detective characters. A review of contemporary crime fiction confirms both its diversity and its diachronic connectedness, after generations of descent from these progenitors. In his discussion, Fishelov notes some "sociopsychological implications" relating to the appropriateness of the family resemblance analogy for the novel in particular; these remarks apply equally accurately to the genre of crime fiction, namely that "the dialectics of imitation and innovation within a generic tradition may be taken as analogous to the parent-child relationship, or to growing up within a family" (2).

Growing up within a family may also lead to rebellion and disaffection with traditions, regardless of the status of the ancestors, and to decisions which may lead members of a family to evolve in ways that depart from expectations and which also lead to descendents whose traits are at considerable variance with previous generations. This is apparent in crime fiction, with its array of sub-genres and whose dominant form has become the novel. Parts of Chandler's 1944 essay, "The Simple Art of Murder" (222-237) – in which his attitude towards the British mystery is frequently both humorously condescending and dismissive – highlight Tynyanov's "broken" evolutionary lines. The essay reminds us, through Chandler's references to Hammett's Black Mask magazine stories and, later, his novels of the 1920s and 1930s, of hybridisation in action, as the former Pinkerton's detective (Gregory 3) applies his knowledge and experience of real-life investigative practices to imaginary crimes and creates the private eye. As Chandler illustrates, Hammett inverted the conventions of the British mystery story, as practised by Christie, among others, moving murder from stable, closed, 'cosy' and centred communities such as St Mary Mead – in which amateur sleuth Marple moved ahead of the police to solve the clue-puzzle and restore equilibrium – to the decentred, unstable world of the twentieth-century's rapid-growth metropolis. In this environment, where sleaze and corruption flourished, the private eye, such as Spade, can never be certain of friends or enemies, or that the next murder won't be his own. No such uncertainty or edginess challenged Marple, whose adventures continued unabated in an 'unrealistic' world which, according to Chandler, depicted "puppets and cardboard lovers and papier mâché villains and detectives of exquisite and impossible gentility"(232). Meanwhile, Spade, Marlowe and their imitators trod their reliably unreliable, and 'realistic' mean streets on the other side of the Atlantic.

All these investigators, regardless of geography, social environment, gender, or personality, are also members of one generic family: crime fiction, and the texts in which they appear are reflective of Fishelov's genre definition. They demonstrate and develop varying approaches to the same problem: investigating and solving crimes, while relying on a core set of skills traceable to Poe's Dupin, the prototypical investigator with superior observational and interpretive abilities. Dupin's direct fictional forebear is the nameless narrator of an earlier Poe story, "The Man of the Crowd" who, as discussed in chapter two, is based on the flâneur, a character which appeared in the mid-nineteenth century in stories published in Parisian newspapers. The flâneur represented a reassuring, all-seeing presence in the increasingly densely populated cities, as industrialisation advanced and social, economic, and cultural landscapes changed forever. In sketches and vignettes, this figure, a wanderer among the city crowds, describes his surroundings and the people he sees, with the aim of reassuring readers anxious about the speed and nature of the changes around them, that there is nothing to fear. Further, this phenomenon of urbanisation can be readily understood through the flâneur's observations and descriptions of those he encounters, individuals who are able to be summed up with a label and made safe, so that society in general can similarly be viewed as secure (Brand 37). Poe, with his interest in the unusual and the dark side of human nature, subverts this character to his own purposes in "The Man of the Crowd," so that elements of potential criminal threat, rather than reassurance, are introduced in the character the narrator observes and pursues through the city. A century later, Hammett and Marlowe responded to their social, economic and political milieux, subverted the roles of Holmesian and Golden Age investigators and created their own twentieth-century descendants of Poe's flâneur-like figure, the innovative private eye.

At this point in the development of the genre, American authors generally, like their colleagues elsewhere in the West, were coming to grips with writing about the urbanised landscapes of their major cities, such as New York, Chicago, San Francisco, and Los Angeles, and their effects on their populations before, during and after the Great Depression, and in the lead-up to World War Two. Some of those who wrote popular fiction and crime stories helped push the genre through its next evolutionary stages. After the early ground-breaking work of Poe and Doyle, the British-style, or Golden Age mystery story and the simultaneously developing American private-eye story were joined, from the 1930s on, and over the next several decades, as Stephen Knight chronicles, by an increasing range of other sub-genres such as the courtroom drama (Erle Stanley Gardner's lawyer, Perry Mason), the police procedural (Lawrence Treat's detective Mitch Taylor, Maurice Procter's Detective Inspector Martineau, and Ed McBain's 87th Precinct stories, offer early examples), the psycho-thriller (Highsmith's Ripley series), the serial-killer (Thomas Harris's killers including Hannibal Lecter), and the foren-sic-investigative novel (most recently popularised by Patricia Cornwell with her Scarpetta series). (Note 5: Knight's Crime Fiction 1800-2000: Detection, Death, Diversity, from which I draw some of these examples, provides a comprehensive history of crime fiction).

Further, political, economic, and social upheaval in Western democracies in the second half of the twentieth century, facilitated the emergence of feminist, gay, black, Jewish, American-Indian, and other demographically-diverse protagonists in investigative roles. In this essay, following the lead of some major critics and analysts, I have grouped all these sub-genres beneath the umbrella title, crime fiction.

C IS FOR CRIME FICTION

Crime fiction is a major contributor to – and certainly in its structure, according to theorists such as Tzvetan Todorov – the novel's position as the dominant literary genre in the West. In terms of sales, Knight quotes a global estimate of up to one-third of the fiction published in English as being crime fiction (x). But what is crime fiction? How is it constituted? What are its 'structural, thematic and functional criteria?' A self-referential genre of the first order, how is it situated relative to other popular and literary genres? Genre fiction is differentiated from literary fiction in terms of its popularity, and crime fiction functions as a form of popular genre fiction. What factors define a text as a member of this genre, using the family resemblance analogy, and bearing in mind Fishelov's definition?

Crime fiction is regarded as genre fiction or popular fiction, its 'opposite' being literary fiction or capital 'L' Literature (the capital distinguishing it from literature generally) (Gelder 12). In its broadest sense, as mentioned earlier, genre falls into three categories: prose, poetry, and drama. Gelder takes prose fiction and divides it into what he calls Literature (using a capital 'L') and popular fiction, the popular fiction genres being crime, romance, science fiction, fantasy, horror, western, adventure and historical popular novels (43). Most readers can identify at least a few of the characteristics or conventions that apply to popular genre texts. In Literature, or literary fiction, generic divisions aren't always so clear, but with popular fiction "generic identities are always visible" (42), and this is the major factor that differentiates it from literary fiction. Gelder proposes that, rather than regard literary and genre/popular fiction as antagonistic – and bearing in mind that there will always be crossover texts – it is more useful to regard them as indispensable to each other in that one cannot exist without the other. As 'opposite' forms of cultural production, literary fiction and genre fiction "need each other for their self-definition. Any form of cultural production, in other words, is dependant upon those features attributed (rightly or wrongly) to the forms from which it distinguishes itself" (13-14).

The "key paradigm" for determining what constitutes popular fiction, according to Gelder, is "industry" (15), whereas literary fiction is measured, not by the prolific abilities of authors to produce large numbers of texts, but by "creativity" (14).   In addition, as Cawelti points out, most literary works are located somewhere between the "mimetic and the formulaic" (13). In other words, texts may be positioned on a continuum that moves from the highly realistic, or mimetic, to the highly idealistic (one might also say artificial), or formulaic. Gelder notes that Literature is traditionally associated with the mimetic end of the continuum, being regarded as "intimately connected with life" and its complexities, whereas popular fiction traditionally "gives itself over to fantasy," is regarded as being simple, and doesn't represent life in a very realistic way (19). But the fact that the extremes of these genres are at opposite ends of a continuum also implies that elements of literary and popular fiction, far from being entirely mutually exclusive, can meet in works that are regarded as both literary fiction – with its attendant creative origins and deeper complexities – and which also become popular by adopting the conventions, methodologies and structures of popular genre fiction. A significant degree of accessibility is also present in enabling this move into what Gelder terms Popular Literature (11). Both Dorothy Porter's verse-novel The Monkey's Mask, and Miss Smilla's Feeling for Snow, by Høeg, for example, are literary texts that have assumed the conventions of the popular sub-genres of the private-eye and amateur sleuth novels respectively, to tell their stories. Miss Smilla is also illustrative of the hybrid text within crime fiction, containing elements of another sub-genre of the thriller that involves the international intrigue of a scientific cover-up that could affect the entire world. Both novels achieved high sales relative to the markets in which they were published. Relatively high sales, while generally the case, aren't invariably so for popular fiction, and it is important to distinguish between popularity as indicated by sales figures and the elements that identify a work as a member of a popular genre, the attributes and conventions that readers look for when they select a text.

Readers approach texts with expectations based on their prior reading experiences and reading relationships with authors and, as Fowler suggests, "readers learn genres gradually, usually through unconscious familiarization" (qtd. in D. Chandler np), and certainly through the conscious acquisition of clues signifying both generic relatedness and difference. As I discuss in chapter two, even the cover of a novel, including its title, offers coded messages to a reader about what to expect (Dubrow 1-3). A simple example would be Q Is for Quarry. Afficionadoes of the private eye sub-genre would recognize the alphabetic reference as indicative of another in the series of novels by Sue Grafton featuring investigator, Kinsey Millhone. Those unfamiliar with the series or the sub-genre would be likely to suspect, at the very least, that 17 other novels, featuring A to P, may have preceded this one. But unless the title was something like M Is for Murder, the title Q Is for Quarry (despite its implied suggestion of a target), in the absence of other markers, could equally be read as indicative of a children's text along the lines of Sesame Street-style acquisition of knowledge about the alphabet and words. But further clues coming to light, such as other features of the cover and the number of pages, guide the reader towards the notion of crime fiction, of a series-based novel with recurring characters. One of these characters is the featured protagonist and investigator ("Another Kinsey Millhone mystery"), a qualified private eye who will, most assuredly, live to fight on in R Is for Richochet, because that is another of the conventions of some crime series: the main character may be subjected to as many life-threatening situations as the author can create, but will survive, no matter what. This is a challenge to the maintenance of suspense, which is offset by its appeal to the reader on another level of expectation: the desire for comfort, in this case, the comfort of knowing that the hero will prevail.

Part of this sense of comfort is based in another identifiable convention related to the structure of many crime fiction texts and, in particular, investigator-based texts featuring some kind of detective – whether professional or non-professional – acting as an individual agent or as a member of a detecting team, as in the police procedural. In his essay, "The Typology of Detective Fiction," Todorov points out that the basis of the 'whodunit' is a duality, and the Russian Formalists identified this double narrative as part of every literary work, separating the fable or story from the subject or plot of the narrative (45). The way the detective novel combines these present and absent stories has led Peter Brooks to theorise it as the "narrative of narratives, its classic structure a laying-bare of the structure of all narrative in that it dramatizes the role of sjuzet (inquest) and fabula (crime) and the nature of their relation" (25).

The detective story contains, in effect, two stories, one present in, and one absent from the narrative, and these equate to the story of the investigation, and the story of the crime (Todorov, Introduction 44). The story of the crime is the "hidden narrative – the story both lived and concealed by the murderer" (Knight 91), and the job of the protagonist-investigator, on behalf of the reader, is to reconstruct the crime by gathering evidence and clues and to return, through the present investigative narrative to the moment of the murder. At this point, some kind of order may be restored, through the exposure and explanation of the murderer's hidden story, and their capture. The level of comfort present in a given text will depend to an extent on the sub-genre it belongs to. Christie's clue-puzzles, for instance, are far more likely to offer a higher level of comfort in their resolutions in the sense that society is stable again (superficially, at least) once the murderer is caught, than that offered by the capture of the latest serial killer in Cornwell's Scarpetta series. Even when a psychopath is captured, one is made aware of the fact that there are many more (with superior intellects a match for any ratiocinative detective) at large, simply waiting in the queue and, furthermore, their killing sprees are random and take place in a de-centred, already destabilised urban world, with none of the certainties present in St Mary Mead.

These conventions help form what Hans Robert Jauss refers to as a reader's "horizon of expectations," which is constituted from "out of a tradition or series of previously known works, and from a specific attitude, mediated by one (or more) genre and dissolved through new works" (79). As Jauss argues, every work belongs to a genre and is defined by its "alterity," or "relation to another, an understanding consciousness" (79). We may say that a reader acquires knowledge of genres both consciously and unconsciously, and applies this knowledge to each new work, comparing it with others both for consistency and originality, testing its acceptability as part of the genre or sub-genre they favour, determining how it resembles or differs from the other members of the textual family that form the genre. The genre category 'crime fiction' is an accommodating and flexible term, suggestive of the limits of its content, and of its capacity for innovation and evolution within these limitations. Like any term employed to describe a genre, it suggests its own 'horizon of expectations,' but how might this horizon be interpreted?

From some perspectives, crime fiction is an overly encompassing term; from others it refers to a particular sub-genre. Malmgren's study, Anatomy of Murder, uses the term 'murder fiction' to include the mystery (or clue-puzzle in the tradition of Christie), the detective story (essentially, the private eye sub-genre created by Chandler and Hammett), and crime fiction (an "oppositional discourse" in which the narrative unfolds from the point of view of the criminal, as in the work of Highsmith). Towards the end of his study, Malmgren discusses the emergence of the police procedural sub-genre from a combination of elements of mystery and detective fiction, transferred to an institutional setting stressing collective over individual agency, to demonstrate the hybrid nature of murder fiction (171-73). Clearly, though, his use of 'murder fiction' excludes all stories in which crimes other than murder are the main focus of the narrative. Others, such as Kathleen Gregory Klein, begin by highlighting that genre is very difficult to define, arguing that most genres demonstrate the qualities of a rubber band, stretching and contracting, twisting and turning this way and that (8). Klein herself applies terms such as 'mystery' fiction and 'detective' fiction interchangeably at times, dispensing with Malmgren's specific differentiation on the basis of their representations of centred and decentred worlds respectively, as he equates them with the British clue-puzzle, cosy form (mystery) and the hard-boiled, American private-eye form (detective). Knight acknowledges the variety of terms sometimes employed to describe the entire genre: detective, mystery, or thriller fiction, for instance. In response to Malmgren's interpretation, Knight applies the term "crime novel" rather than "crime fiction" to denote works where the point of view of the criminal is adopted. Detective or mystery fiction fall short, Knight argues, in that not all novels described as such incorporate a detective (some of Christie's: Ordeal by Innocence, The Secret of Chimneys) or even a mystery (most of Highsmith's work), and the word 'thriller' is too "simply emotive," being more useful as part of 'psychothriller' to emphasise the "disturbing excitement" the term conjures. Knight chooses crime fiction as the overarching term, his primary requirement for membership being that a crime occurs, or at least the appearance of a crime (xii-xiii).

Knight's definition, with its nod to boundaries and conventions, and with its tacit invitation to consider innovation and evolution, is the one I employ in this essay, and rightly includes stories in which murder may not figure at all, although it is the case – and

Malmgren's term, murder fiction, acknowledges this – that the crime du jour in the overwhelming majority of contemporary crime fiction texts, as I discuss in chapter three, is murder. Further, in terms of my focus on the sub-genres that provide investigator-based murder novels, this definition allows, within its horizon of expectations, for the pursuit of a solution involving an investigation incorporating the capture of the criminal and the exposure and explanation of the absent or concealed story, as far as this may be possible, as the unifying basis of the narrative. It thus makes possible the delineation and foregrounding of the character roles of investigator, victim, and suspects in the narrative, and the ways in which these roles contribute to a custom fit text.

*

In this chapter, I introduce three alternative perspectives on character roles and characterisation strategies in investigator-based murder novels: the proximal investigator, the corpse of convenience, and the family of circumstance. I also provide a context in which these alternatives may be discussed by proposing definitions of genre and of the specific genre of crime fiction, within which murder novels may be found across a variety of sub-genres. I suggest an analogy with which crime fiction may be compared to confirm its hybrid nature and its ability to evolve in response to social, historical, and cultural challenges. In the following chapters, I employ selected texts to discuss and illustrate the ways in which authors attempt to achieve a custom fit through character roles and characterisation strategies, and so provide a 'same but different' reading experience.

In the next chapter, "Reinventing the Unique: The Proximal Investigator in Series and One-Off Murder Novels," I analyse the concept of proximity as it is embodied in the character of the investigator in order to better understand the strategies adopted by selected authors in creating and developing their protagonists. I remove the labels that differentiate the investigator types appearing in various sub-genres of murder fiction, substituting the term 'proximal investigator' as I define it at the beginning of this chapter. In so doing, my goal is to clarify a range of differences and similarities in these characters and better understand the nature of their relationships and the positions they occupy in their narratives.

In chapter three, "Death and the Family: Two Key Sites of Criminal Proximity," I consider approaches to death as it is depicted in contemporary murder fiction, my departure point being Atwood's assertion that all narrative is motivated by a fear of our mortality. I ask if it's possible to construct a continuum of emotional involvement, along which one might position any victim from murder texts, based on the level of convenience that a particular corpse lends to a narrative structure against the emotional investment in the victim demonstrated by other characters in the story and by how the victim is portrayed. What level of care is present in murder fiction for the corpse of convenience, and what does this character contribute to the custom fit text?

Following this, I consider the family of circumstance, of whom the corpse of convenience is a key member. Without the corpse, the narrative and its cast don't exist. I consider the ways in which families of circumstance, consisting of the proximal investigator's family of origin and family of choice within the family of suspects, interrelate to differentiate one murder novel from another in meaningful ways. But first, I return to the character that is the most important contributor to a 'same but different' reading experience in murder novels, the proximal investigator.

CHAPTER TWO

Reinventing the Unique: The Proximal Investigator in Series and One-Off Murder Novels

... it is (still) the time that we spend with characters that matters most to many readers.
Deidre Shauna Lynch, The Economy of Character 1

This chapter considers the emergence of early proximal investigators, together with the ways portrayals of proximal investigators in contemporary murder novels offer a 'same but different' reading experience. In employing this term to de-emphasise the taxonomic labels of private eye, forensic medical examiner, police detective, amateur, and so on, with their accompanying investigative conventions, assumptions, and masks, my aim is to foreground, through the lens of characterisation, some other topics present in much contemporary crime fiction. On one level, the word 'proximal' reminds us that the investigator may be, or may become, physically, familially, vocationally, or in some other way communally near to or associated with the subject of the criminal activity: the homicide victim or victims, for instance. Other topics are also embedded in the narrative and embodied in the person of the investigator, who acts as a conduit for the exploration of social, political, economic, racial, and gender-based issues and themes, among others. These are what I call the sites of proximity, or the proximate issues that inform and underpin the narrative. Other scholars, such as Karin Molander Danielsson, employ the term 'special interest' in a similar way to designate such sites; part of her focus is on whether or not special interest texts risk becoming too exclusive, relative to their initial positioning as members of a popular genre like detective fiction. Some authors of these texts, as discussed below, Paretsky and Mankell, for example, have no qualms about confirming that their creations, Warshawski and Wallander, each co-exist as investigators and eloquent mouthpieces for their respective social and political opinions. While they may risk accusations of ideological bias, this is also part of their appeal to their audiences. Certainly, criticisms relating to perceived biases can be found on internet fan sites in web logs, or blogs, discussing popular authors' offerings. This is part of the discussion a novel may naturally provoke. There are frequently as many readers in favour of representing political views in detective novels, such as Paretsky's Blacklist, for instance, which includes discussion of the McCarthy era, the Patriot Act, homophobia, and race relations, as there are against such topics.

Engaging with Warshawski and Wallander as proximal investigators, and then with their masks in place as private investigator and police detective, is another way in which their readers, and critics, can gain a fuller sense of who these characters are, and why their audiences return again and again for further variations on a theme. "Endless repetition," as Martin Priestman reminds us, "is, of course, the soul of the series as a form" (93), but there is more to this reading experience than the comfort of repetition. Conan Doyle recognised the power of a single, compelling character running through a series to attract a loyal readership and claims to have been the first to publish, in the Strand magazine, self-contained stories featuring an ongoing character, Holmes (95-96), who was his response to Émile Gaboriau's neatly dovetailed plots and Poe's detective, Dupin (74). Contemporary series writers, like Paretsky, include both her investigator and the investigator's family of circumstance, taking "pleasure in developing a set of people in detail, showing the progression of their lives, not abandoning them at one climax when we all know most lives have many pivot points" ("Writing" 59). In her Warshawski novels, Paretsky foregrounds characterisation and, through her characters, maintains an ongoing, complex engagement with successive detective plots and her chosen sites of proximity.

In considering the evolution of the proximal investigator, I next discuss the origins of the character of the investigator and, in particular, the amateur. I illustrate the diversity and sheer volume of authors operating in the genre with examples from contemporary investigator-based murder novels. Milan Kundera argues that "all novels, of every age, are concerned with the enigma of the self. As soon as you create an imaginary being, a character, you are automatically confronted by the question: What is the self?" (23). Increasingly, the success of these texts is related to the added attention authors give to character development by privileging protagonists' private lives and by incorporating many other issues, or sites of proximity, into their plots with which the protagonists can engage. A sense of the evolution of character roles and strategies reinforces the nature of genres as dynamic, adaptable entities and, at the same time, confirms Todorov's assertion that the detective story's plot structure, 'the narrative of narratives,' is robust enough – its relative rigidity positively encourages challenges – to survive and thrive in the face of evolutionary change and hybridisation. Finally, I note some significant and differentiating character traits of the proximal investigators, and highlight sites of proximity in novels by Høeg, Walter Mosley, Mankell, and Paretsky, which represent four different investigator/ protagonist roles – the amateur (two variations in the works of Høeg and Mosley), the police detective, and the private eye. The custom fit text is embodied in the murder novels of each of these authors.

EARLY PROXIMAL INVESTIGATORS: C. AUGUSTE DUPIN AND HIS SUCCESSORS

The contemporary investigator-based murder text in which a dedicated investigator, exploiting their power of independent agency, follows a series of clues to reconstruct a crime and reveal the killer, has its origins in mid-nineteenth century American literature. The amateur investigator or detective evolved from the short stories of Poe (Priestman 36; Binyon 4), beginning with "The Murders in the Rue Morgue" in 1841. Although the word 'detective' was unknown at that time (Symons 34), Poe's character, Dupin, emerges as "the first intellectual detective" (Knight 209), who relies on ratiocination, or superior powers of observation, analysis, logic, and deduction to solve the crimes presented to him. In the case of the "Rue Morgue," a story narrated by an observing friend along the lines of Dr Watson in the Holmes stories, Dupin rightly concludes, through a complicated series of observations, deductions, and entrapment, that an orang-utan murdered the victims – two women, a mother and her daughter – in an apparently locked room, a crime for which an innocent man is initially arrested.

Dupin was prefigured in an earlier Poe story, "The Man of the Crowd," in which the narrator, a man recovering from an illness, finds himself on a particular day feeling "a calm but inquisitive interest in every thing" (164) and an "absorption in contemplation of the scene without" (164), as he sits in the bow-window of the D____ Coffee House in London watching the world go by. This is similar to the situation of the flâneur, a popular figure in stories and sketches of the era, which appeared in the feuilletons, the cultural and entertainment sections of Parisian newspapers in the 1830s (Brand 37). (Note 6: My emphasis in this essay is on Poe's engagement with this figure as a forerunner to the detective character, but there are interesting analyses of the flâneur in The Flâneur, a collection of essays edited by Keith Tester. Walter Benjamin discusses Baudelaire's poetry on this figure in Charles Baudelaire:A Lyric Poet in the Era of High Capitalism). Flâneurs, as mentioned in chapter one, strolled or idled in and around urban crowds in the growing cities, describing what they saw with the aim of reassuring readers that people and their behaviour in these increasingly populous and complex urban landscapes – a source of anxiety for many citizens – could be easily described and understood, labelled and typed. "If everyone was legible and classifiable," as Dana Brand notes in her essay derived from Walter Benjamin's analysis of the flâneur and Poe's invention of the detective story, "no one could be terribly threatening. In the city of the flâneur, even criminals could be thought of as transparent, predictable, and ultimately amusing" (37). But Poe, she suggests, used the flâneur's style of sketch to create a new kind of narrative, the detective story, offering "new and more complex illusions of urban legibility than those offered by the flâneur" and "new opportunities to exploit the public fascination with those aspects of urban life the flâneur attempts to deny" (36).

Initially in Poe's story of a flâneur-like observer, a general level of observation gives way to a keener interest in details, "the innumerable varieties of figure, dress, air, gait, visage, and expression of countenance"(164). He notes a range of characters – gamblers, clerks, pick-pockets – and though time passes, night falls, and the street darkens, he is able to read, with only a glance at the faces passing by his window seat, "the history of long years" (166), demonstrating his facility as a flâneur, and more. Eventually, though, he sees a face to which he is attracted by virtue of "the idiosyncrasy of its expression" (167). He sees in this man the face of a "fiend," and it provokes in him a range of impressions: intelligence, greed, calmness, fear, viciousness, and "supreme despair" (167). He notices that the man carries both a diamond and a dagger and implies that his clothes, though now in a state of disrepair, are made from an expensive fabric, which marks him as perhaps having once been a person of class and means. He has assumed the role of the Other, the 'fiend' beyond the control of society's conventions and laws. His apparent fall from grace may offer a further source of anxiety, a disruption of the social order at a time when organised institutional policing was in its infancy. The narrator is confused and unaccountably attracted by the man's appearance and demeanour; he wants to know more as he follows him, undetected, through the streets of London, moving from crowd to crowd throughout the night, seemingly addicted to being among people, unable, the narrator concludes, to contemplate being alone. In the final part of the story, he follows the man to "the most noisome quarter of London, where every thing wore the worst impress of the most deplorable poverty, and of the most desperate crime"(169). We have moved out of the flâneur's comfort zone; the narrator, turned gumshoe, has arrived at the dark underside of the city, and here, again, his 'person of interest,' the potential criminal, disappears into a "huge suburban temple of Intemperance:" a gin palace (169). But before long, the pub closes and as dawn breaks, the man leaves, and the cycle begins again, with the narrator in pursuit throughout another day, returning, finally, to the site of his first encounter with the man who remains, despite the narrator's attentions, passionate interest, and tracking expertise, unknown and ultimately, despite the narrator staring at him "steadfastly in the face" (169), unknowable. He represents, for the narrator, who is in no doubt, "'the type and the genius of deep crime. He refuses to be alone. He is the man of the crowd. It will be in vain to follow; for I shall learn no more of him, nor of his deeds'" (169).

We learn no more about the man of the crowd which, in itself, is unsettling as we are left to wonder about his true potential as a criminal and his capacity to upset the social order. The narrator takes refuge in the thought that a merciful God ensures that daylight approaches and the darkness of evening will lift. Along with light comes the prospect of safety and perhaps a kind of resolution, albeit an unsatisfactory one. A further source of dissatisfaction is that we have learned little about the narrator of the story other than that he is a convalescent speedily recovering his physical strength and acute powers of observation, qualities that allow him to confront his urban environment beyond its superficial sheen. The narrator evolves into Dupin, investigator – initially via newspaper reports – in "The Murders in the Rue Morgue," a story that includes, as Dorothy L. Sayers points out (60), many elements of later detective stories of the nineteenth and twentieth centuries: an apparently locked room, the

arrest of an innocent suspect, evidence missed by the police but discovered by a superior investigator with his special feeling for the
case and perceptive analysis of the clues, all of which leads to solving
the mystery of the women's deaths. And, although these deaths were
caused by an animal rather than by a human committing homicide,
the story prefigures, in a somewhat bizarre way, the gradual move
from a concentration on the depiction of crimes against property in
nineteenth century short stories, and novels such as Wilkie Collins's
The Moonstone (featuring some of the earliest police detective characters), to murder as the offence of choice in the early twentieth
century and onwards. Knight suggests several reasons for this
change of focus, including an increasing interest, in the late nineteenth century, in stories of the "grisly" and the "sensational," by
writers such as Bram Stoker (Dracula 1897) and Robert Louis Stevenson (The Strange Case of Dr Jekyll and Mr Hyde 1886), and a
move away from an "obsession with property as the core of respect-
able life" towards "a central importance of the identity of the self, and
threats towards it" (67-68). It is a change which remains very much
in evidence in contemporary crime fiction and which supports the
continuing success and evolution of sub-genres that feature strong,
resilient, courageous main characters whose flaws and frailties are
also exposed as they develop and face the life-, love- and relation-
ship-threatening challenges of their professional and personal lives.

But this change in the representation of character roles has taken
the better part of the twentieth century to develop. In both "The
Murders in the Rue Morgue" and "The Man of the Crowd," we also
note characteristics of the hard-boiled private eyes created by Hammett (Spade) and Chandler (Marlowe). The narrator in "The Man of
the Crowd," a man who is "himself not mean" ("Simple" 237) makes

his way through some of the meaner streets of London, observant, stealthy, for the most part concealed, conducting his 'investigation.' His successor, Dupin, is a loner, encouraged by his new friend, the story's narrator, to engage with the mystery of the women's deaths. Both characters possess unusual qualities as investigators, but they are not what one would describe as fully-realised, in keeping with the early era of crime fiction and, indeed, with much contemporary crime fiction.

Characters such as Dupin, Conan Doyle's Holmes, Christie's Marple and Hercule Poirot, G. K. Chesterton's Father Brown, and others, demonstrate strange skills and gifts, a few personal peculiarities, and are established, by and large, as amateur detectives par excellence, memorable for their unique ability to reconstruct and solve puzzling, complex crimes. As readers, we are convinced that this character, Holmes, after a snort of cocaine and playing a Bach violin concerto, is the only "professional amateur" (Binyon 6) investigator who can solve this case. We are certain that this so-called "amateur amateur" (7), Marple, is the one who will, before an afternoon of gardening, and with the offer of tea and scones perhaps, outwit the criminals and the police. She will restore order and a new status quo to village life and, therefore, restore safety. At a certain level, Marple or Dupin reconstruct clues and evidence to achieve the same goal as forensic medical examiner, Scarpetta, when she deconstructs a human body in order to observe and reveal the elements of criminal trespass, except that, as Peter Messent notes, Scarpetta has the supplementary advantage of advanced forensic technology and scientific skills (13). The investigators' possession of specialist skills, whether or not they are classified as amateurs, and their proximity to the circumstances of the crime, their pre-existing or developing relationship with the victim and the suspects ensures that the aim is the same: resolution, the restoration of a new equilibrium, the solution to the puzzle.

It is the puzzle and its solution that dictated the importance of plotting and structure, and which equally ensured that the protagonists of the early decades of crime fiction, should they turn side-on and obscure their few remarkable features – unmistakable though these were – would largely disappear from view. Willard Huntington Wright argues that the detective story is essentially a riddle, a "complicated and extended puzzle" which he compares to the crossword puzzle. Clues are provided, the boundaries of the puzzle are clearly delineated, and one must deliberate over, and analyse the clues to determine how they fit together. A soupçon of speculation and guesswork isn't out of the question in order to bridge gaps in one's knowledge, but at the end, when the solution is reached, "all the details are found to be woven into a complete, interrelated, and closely knitted fabric" (35-36). Much less attention is given to characterisation because, Wright suggests, "there is no more stimulating activity than that of the mind; and there is no more exciting adventure than that of the intellect" (36). Although he allows that the main character, the investigator, is the "outstanding" personality of the story, he only participates in it in an "ex parte" capacity, acting on behalf of others as a narrative guide (40). The investigator is, essentially, an element of the plot, important, but ultimately subservient to the puzzle which is constructed in accordance with agreed rules.

Writing in 1928 under the pseudonym of S. S. Van Dine, Wright produced a set of 22 rules for writing detective stories – based on his reading of hundreds of such stories while he recovered from an illness – and identifying the recurring conventions they contained. In these rules, he reinforces the view that characterisation isn't of great significance. Taken as a whole, the rules, while tinged with humour and even hints of irony, provide a useful illustration of genre rigidity. The fact that they were written is a demonstration of the power of genre, as is the fact that they are one of a number of examples of sets of rules or directives proffered by practitioners and critics over many years, some of them more prominent than others, such as Ronald A. Knox, and, more recently, Elmore Leonard. The earlier lists from Van Dine and Knox also remind us of a conscious intention on the part of previous generations of crime authors not to engage with issues – including in-depth characterisation – other than those which were strictly puzzle-worthy and which contributed to the solution.

The beginning of Van Dine's rule number 16 is the direct opposite of some of the major preoccupations of the contemporary crime novel. It is worth quoting here, because I soon move to discuss contemporary protagonists and the establishment of their status as proximal investigators and of certain sites of proximity. It also serves as a reminder of Tynyanov's argument, discussed in chapter one, that genres are evolutionary in nature, and as an indicator of their hybrid vigour:

> 16. A detective novel should contain no long descriptive passages, no literary dallying with side-issues, no subtly worked-out character analyses, no "atmospheric" preoccupations. Such matters have no vital place in a record of crime and deduction. They hold up the action, and introduce issues irrelevant to the main purpose, which is to state a problem, analyze it, and bring it to a successful conclusion. To be sure, there must be a sufficient descriptiveness

and character delineation to give the novel verisimilitude. (191-92)

The nature of investigator-based crime fiction has changed significantly since Van Dine published his rules, not because the main purpose has changed radically, but because authors, readers, and publishers have come to demand more and different approaches as social, political, and economic conditions change, and influence fiction generally. The world has changed and so has the genre. At the same time as the concerns of crime fiction's proximal investigators have broadened beyond the pursuit of criminals and justice for the victims so, too, have the sites of proximity increased and diversified. "Atmospheric" preoccupations; loving, incisive, critical, or outraged descriptions of cityscapes and landscapes; "dallying with side-issues;" the nature and tone of climatic conditions and the accompanying qualities of light; and subtle, deeply-felt characterisation, these elements Van Dine proscribed, are commonplace in contemporary crime fiction. The disequilibrium facing the investigator – who is more, rather than less, likely to lack self-confidence, unlike the definite and definitive Dupin – and the affected community, has many sources, apart from the primary commission of a murder. These sources are acknowledged, represented, and analysed as the pursuit unfolds. The character of the contemporary proximal investigator is increasingly a conduit by which the elements Van Dine regarded as irrelevant have established themselves as commonplace, as essential to the internal verisimilitude of the text, and as accepted conventions of the genre.

CONTEMPORARY PROXIMAL INVESTIGATORS

Contemporary investigator-based murder texts are typologised and marketed on the basis of their protagonists, the investigators: private eyes, police detectives, and forensic experts, medical examiners, bounty hunters, and amateurs. Their authors pay significant attention to creating and developing them as people with lives – relationships, pre-occupations, challenges – outside their investigatory activities. The best of them are more than sketchy or two-dimensional characters memorable for behavioural or intellectual quirks such as cocaine addiction or outrageously superior observational skills. They cover a broad and diverse demography; they are realistically portrayed, and likely to reflect the contemporary issues and challenges facing their readers (DellaCava and Engel 1). They appear in one-off and series texts, although the series is the preferred option of many authors. Paretsky, for example, likes the idea of a series because it allows her to develop a group of characters over a longer period of time, and to "explore a set of issues from the same perspective" ("Writing" 59) and, as Danielsson argues, "the text that can combine a special interest and an interesting character has a considerable rhetorical power" (180).

In the case of a series, once a writer's proximal investigator achieves a measure of success, defined by volume of sales and publication of further instalments, cover blurbs often acknowledge the fact by exhorting readers to experience "Scarpetta at Her Blistering Best" (Point of Origin, by Cornwell), and "Vintage Scarpetta" (Unnatural Exposure). More conservative announcements, some of them confined to the title page, simply state: "The New Kinsey Millhone Mystery" (S is for Silence, by Grafton), or "The New Lincoln Rhyme Thriller" (The Empty Chair, by Jeffery Deaver), or "An

Elvis Cole novel" (L.A. Requiem, by Robert Crais). Simple, but effective, it tells the reader what they want to know: they've been here before with this character, but the mystery is new, the title a tease, and Kay or Kinsey or Lincoln or Elvis will see them through the chaos to a successful apprehension of the killer or killers and the restoration of order. Along the way, we will learn more about these characters, about their relationships and their worlds, about what shapes their attitudes, and how they respond to their circumstances. Where a lighter touch is required and chaos, or chronic disequilibrium, is frequently the norm, a way of life to be embraced rather than something to be dealt with and resolved, the reader may be invited to "Take a walk on the wild side with the world's favourite bounty hunter, Stephanie Plum," for the tenth time (Ten Big Ones), but who's counting? We, the readers are counting, as are publishers and writers, each of them for their own reasons. Some of these reasons may be represented in single words as stepping-off points for discussion which is beyond my scope in this essay: entertainment (readers), profit (publishers), and industry (writers). As Gelder observes in relation to these issues, "serialization secures a loyal readership and consolidates a novelist's reputation" (16). It is clearly the case though, that not every crime writer needs to write a series to secure a massive readership, as authors like Minette Walters, Harlan Coben, and Robert Goddard have proven with a succession of one-off novels featuring non-recurring protagonists.

In the case of one-off texts, the protagonist's name may form part of the title, as in Miss Smilla's Feeling for Snow. In this somewhat mysterious title, the implication is that Miss Smilla's intuition, her 'feeling' for snow, somehow qualifies her as an investigator: she possesses a special, innate ability that will be deployed in the novel in pursuit of the truth. Before a page is turned in the one-off text or the series instalment, the reader of murder fiction is offered clues to what lies between the covers. Inexperienced readers of the genre can glean something from the cover of a crime novel, even if the something leads only to a question or, more encouragingly, to several questions. But with these questions come the expectation of answers to be provided within by their favourite investigators.

The cover is at the forefront of the fulfilment of the reader's 'horizon of expectations,' their accumulation of knowledge about how to read and interpret texts written in accordance with the conventions, rules, and parameters of a particular genre. The cover provides a coded message heralding a particular kind of reading experience. Including the name of the investigator on the cover is likely to conjure an already familiar picture of a dedicated police detective at a messy (or tidy) desk in a high-rise office, or a forensic medical examiner at an autopsy table with a corpse and a Stryker saw; a hard-boiled private eye in a down-at-heel inner-city suburb wondering how to pay the lease, or a former lingerie saleswoman watching her latest automobile explode and erupt into flames. As readers, we imagine our favourite investigators in their special roles, and feel a level of comfort that our expectations will be fulfilled, but in a slightly different way each time. The many sub-genres of crime fiction are accompanied by an enormous variety of protagonists or investigators. The images they suggest to us help us to distinguish them from each other, and to distinguish a 'same but different' reading experience. As modern genre theory suggests, there is no limit to the number of sub-genres that may emerge within crime fiction, which has and continues to develop on "the basis of inclusiveness or

'richness' as well as that of 'purity' (genre by accretion as well as reduction)" (Wellek and Warren 234).

As one scans bibliographic studies, library catalogue search results, and web-site lists, it can seem that there is a sub-genre, or sub-
sub-genre investigator to cater for every crime fiction reading taste.
The main characters in today's crime fiction have moved beyond the
white, male, heterosexual police detective or private eye or amateur,
though he is still very much in evidence as Cliff Hardy, Scobie
Malone, Chief Inspector Wexford, and Commander Adam Dalgliesh
demonstrate. A glance at bookshop or library shelves, or any recent
surveys of crime fiction reveal that, in the United States, for example
– one of the biggest crime fiction markets in the world – the 'alternative' male competition is prolific and includes an alcoholic Greek-
American (Nick Stefanos, written by George Pelecanos), a quadri-
plegic African-American forensic expert (Deaver's Lincoln Rhyme),
a gay insurance claims investigator and private eye (Joseph Hansen's
Dave Brandstetter), an African-American amateur detective operating in 1940s and 1950s Los Angeles (Mosley's Ezekiel 'Easy'
Rawlins), and a Jewish-American rabbi (David Small, written by
Harry Kemelman), among dozens of police, private and amateur
investigators with unusual backgrounds and motivations. (Note 7:
There is an interesting sidebar to the Kemelman novels in which
David Small, the rabbi and main character, is assisted by his wife,
Rachel, and the Chief of Police, Hugh Lanigan. A short-lived televi-
sion series, based on the novels, aired in 1977 in the United States.
In The History of Mystery, Max Collins reports that the television
show, named Lanigan's Rabbi, moved the setting from Massachu-
setts to California, "played down the Judaism" and, as the title sug-

gests, gave primary status and top billing to the Catholic police chief (100)).

The field is no longer dominated by male investigators as it once was, however, and it is important to note that female detectives have been active in crime fiction since the 1860s (Craig and Cadogan 11), with one of the most popular investigators of all time the elderly Miss Marple. (Note 8: Agatha Christie's book sales total over two billion copies in 44 languages to 2006, with current royalty earnings estimated at $US 3.7 million per year ("Best"). Miss Marple appears in 17 (and potentially over half a million royalty dollars per year), of Christie's 84 novels and short story collections (Toye 263)). The last quarter of a century, following the second wave of feminism in Western countries since the 1960s, has seen the biggest expansion in the numbers of female characters as primary investigators. Now, women provide a similar variety of characters to their male counterparts. Opening DellaCava and Engel's bibliography of serialised female American sleuths to a random double-page display offers a forensic sculptor from Georgia (Eve Duncan, written by Iris Johansen), a gourmet caterer based in Cincinnati (Cathie John's Kate Cavanaugh), an insurance company investigator in Washington, D. C. (Colleen Fitzgerald, by Barbara Johnson), a Denver dry cleaner, and an astrology columnist from the same city (Mandy Dyer and Jane Smith, by Dolores Johnson and Christine T. Jorgensen, respectively), a Chaucer scholar (D. J. H. Jones's Professor Nancy Ranford Cook), a San Franciscan virologist (B. B. Jordan's Celeste Braun) and, by chance, and in the interests of tradition, a lawyer from Chicago (Rachel Gold, by Michael A. Kahn) (182-83). DellaCava and Engel note that, while 45 female sleuths were written between the

1890s and 1979, since 1980 477 new characters have appeared, and these account only for American investigators (x).

Enumerating and naming some of the thousands of fictional investigators in print today, supports my contention that, with diversity and numbers, and with the increasing attention being paid to character development (and marketing), particularly of the roles of the protagonists, has also come an expansion in the sites of proximity created and explored in these texts. These sites and the role of the proximal investigator may usefully be examined by surveying characterisation strategies employed by four authors whose texts feature two different kinds of amateur, a private eye, and a police inspector, as the proximal investigators. With the broadening of content and attention to Van Dine's "side-issues," comes the potential for writers to achieve deeper characterisation, with its concomitant deepening of reader satisfaction and entertainment. It is a potential that is fulfilled by the writers whose texts I discuss below. The unique, custom-fit quality of each of their proximal investigators contributes to their ability to offer a 'same but different' reading experience and engage successfully with their chosen sites of proximity.

PROXIMAL INVESTIGATORS IN NOVELS BY PETER HØEG, WALTER MOSLEY, HENNING MANKELL, AND SARA PARETSKY

As we have seen, one of the most successful ways of marketing investigator-based murder texts is by highlighting the character of the proximal investigator as unique, as the only agent who is capable of solving the crimes that occur in and around their proximal space. In this section, I consider four proximal investigators who represent the amateur (Høeg's Jaspersen and Mosley's Rawlins, with qualifications), the private eye (Paretsky's Warshawski), and the police detective (Mankell's Wallander), and identify one differentiating, special quality each possesses that sets them apart and contributes towards achieving the goal of creating the custom fit text. I also look at the limiting nature of terms such as amateur when applied to contemporary investigators, to suggest that such terms work against the idea that the protagonist/ investigator possesses both unique crime-solving qualities and is, furthermore, a character worthy of attention for a range of other reasons, including the sites of proximity they visit and explore.

As argued above, since its inception, the character of the investigator has possessed special qualities. Poe's Dupin established the notion of the ratiocinative investigator with superior reasoning and observational skills allowing him to solve crimes that would otherwise remain mysteries if left to the police with their, by definition, less extraordinary powers of detection. These special attributes are present to varying degrees in many of our contemporary proximal investigators, inherited from Dupin through a long line of descendants, including the usual standard-bearers such as Holmes, Marple, Lord Peter Wimsey, Spade, Marlowe, and Ellery Queen. But as noted, many contemporary proximal investigators are more fully-realised, rounded characters as well, capable of significant self-reflection and insight into their own and others' lives. They are people we can imagine existing in the real world. However, for the purpose of their lives as fictional investigators, they must also demonstrate qualities beyond the conventional skills of detection, and beyond the usual range of qualities that make up a personality. From this perspective, to achieve a custom fit in their sub-genre they must provide something extra-special, and the more enduring contemporary proximal investigators appear to fulfill this requirement, although the extra-special applies with equal validity to one-off texts. One of these, Miss Smilla's Feeling for Snow, Høeg's best-selling novel, an example of what Gelder might call Popular Literature, offers, as I mentioned earlier, an illustration of the protagonist's unique asset before a page is turned, in the title. (Note 9: Høeg's novel is translated from the Danish and published under slightly different titles for different English-speaking markets, including Smilla's Sense of Snow in the United States).

Jaspersen can be understood as a custom fit proximal investigator in a number of senses of the term. She is vocationally, communally, geographically, demographically, politically, and personally suited to the investigation of the death of her young neighbour, Isaiah Christiansen. She is a glaciologist living in the same Copenhagen apartment building as Isaiah, and is a Greenlander like him, although her father, Moritz, a prominent and wealthy physician, is Danish, which places her in a relatively privileged position. She has very strong opinions about the Danish government's attitudes, over generations, towards their colony, her home country, and their treatment of Greenlanders as second-class citizens in both Greenland and Denmark. She has become, as Isaiah's neighbour, a friend but also a de facto mother figure, offering him a home when he needs it, taking care of his physical needs to be fed, bathed, and clothed. She develops a meaningful relationship with him that represents an alternative kind of support that isn't available in the impaired relationship he experiences with his alcoholic mother, Juliane. Apart from these factors, Smilla has another, innate quality, her feeling for snow, both an intellectual and an intuitive or sixth sense that takes her knowledge and understanding of snow in all its forms far beyond her formal education as a glaciologist, a profession which has enabled her to participate in scientific expeditions to Greenland. Smilla's ability to read snow first became apparent when she was a child living in her homeland, and she saved her family and village group from death on the ice when they were caught in fog on their way home from a fishing expedition:

> When it happens for the first time, it's like discovering that you're awake while everyone else is sleeping. Equal parts loneliness and omnipotence. We're on our way from Qinnissut to the Inglefield estuary...
>
> For some time we've noticed that fog is on the way, but when it comes, it comes suddenly, like a collective blindness. Even the dogs huddle together. But for me there really isn't any fog. There is a wild, bright feeling of elation, because I know with absolute certainty which way we should go.
>
> My mother listens to me, and the others listen to her. I am placed on the front sleigh, and I can remember feeling that we were driving along a string of silver, stretched between me and the house in Qaanaaq. The instant before the gable appears out of the night, I know that it's there. (37-38)

Smilla's complex relationship with, and knowledge of snow ("I think more highly of snow and ice than of love" [39]), is what enables her to see that Isaiah's footprints, on the roof of the building near their apartment block, have left the wrong kind of imprint for someone who fell accidentally, but rather indicate that he was fleeing from someone, trying to escape. This interpretation, combined with Smilla's knowledge of Isaiah's extreme fear of heights, are two factors that draw her into becoming the novel's proximal investigator.

But there is also, importantly, Smilla's realisation at Isaiah's funeral at the beginning of the novel: "All along, I must have had an extensive pact with Isaiah about not leaving him in the lurch, never, not now either" (4). She acts in the role of an amateur investigator – she is neither a private eye nor a police detective, but her methods echo gumshoe and procedural activities – motivated by her personal relationship with Isaiah, in keeping with the way so many amateurs become involved in cases, and by her suspicions about the hurried police ruling that the boy's death was accidental.

But she brings her extraordinary skills and ruthless determination to the investigation in ways that suggest she is anything but an amateur. Here, with an ideal proximal investigator as illustration, the term amateur may be set aside. The most basic reason for this relates to the word amateur itself, and is rooted in my creation of Livia Galvin as an investigator. Just as Jaspersen is no amateur in relation to her knowledge, formal and instinctive, of snow, neither is Livia an amateur in relation to her family, even with her deliberate efforts to remain at a distance from their criminal activities. She is like every individual who belongs to their own version of this social group, a professional family member: she knows her job and performs it, or aims to perform it in an efficient, effective way, according to her own sense of where she belongs within it. My use of the term proximal investigator has its origins in Livia's proximity to her family, and to Minnie Babitsky. The term expanded to incorporate the notion of sites of proximity, and as its applicability became apparent in relation to other kinds of investigators. But initially, amateur was the best term of those available to describe Livia in the context of how she is portrayed in "Thicker Than Water," and it is a word that is, by its very nature, limiting and limited. While it may suggest the positive idea of a voluntary contribution to the social capital by virtue of its implication of unpaid labour, or pursuing an interest for the love of it, it is a word that has negative and pejorative overtones, with implications of mediocre or second-rate performance when compared with its antonym, professional. In this context, it is more suggestive of weakness than of the strength demonstrated by so many so-called amateur investigators in crime fiction.

The New Shorter Oxford English Dictionary defines an amateur as "a person who is fond of something; a person who has a taste for something ... a person who practices something, especially an art or game, only as a pastime ... a dabbler ... not professional; also (depreciative), unskilful, amateurish"(1: 62-63). Dennis Porter argues that investigator-based crime fiction requires a protagonist with specialist skills to solve the crime in question (5), abilities that surpass dabbling, unskilled fondness, attributes that invite the, admittedly biased, ridicule of Marlowe's creator, Chandler. Chandler regards the Golden Age amateur sleuths as jokes, "detectives of exquisite and impossible gentility" ("Simple" 232), comparing them very unfavorably with the likes of Spade, Hammett's creation. Hammett, after all, according to Chandler, "gave murder back to the kind of people that commit it for reasons, not just to provide a corpse; and with the means at hand, not with hand-wrought duelling pistols, curare, and tropical fish" (234).

Chandler's remarks foreground one of the hierarchies of crime fiction, and the basis of this hierarchical dominance, from Chandler's perspective, is realism, or his construction of realism, which apparently belongs to the private eye, a man who lives in:

> a world in which gangsters can rule nations and almost rule
> cities ... a world where a judge with a cellar full of bootleg
> liquor can send a man to jail for having a pint in his pocket
> ... where no man can walk down a dark street in safety be-
> cause law and order are things we talk about but refrain
> from practising .... It is not a very fragrant world, but it is
> the world you live in, and certain writers with tough minds
> and a cool spirit of detachment can make very interesting
> and even amusing patterns out of it. (236)

Chandler's perspective privileges the sort of verisimilitude (or appearance of authenticity or reality) that compares the content of a fictional text with the so-called real world of lived experience. By this standard, the likes of Marple, amateur sleuth with a spectacular success rate despite this description, fail miserably. How often, in the 'real' world, has a little old lady living in a small English village, solved a murder, and usually in advance of the police? The short answer, in the absence of statistics, is perhaps never and, more certainly, not often. On the other hand, James Ellroy emphatically points out, "the last time a private eye investigated a homicide was never.' The private eye is an iconic totem spawned by pure fiction, romantic moonshine" (qtd. in Messent 11). And how close, after all, would a contemporary private investigator even get to a murder investigation? Not very close, according to Joyce Carol Oates, who argues that "'private detectives are rarely involved in authentic crime cases, and would have no access, in contemporary times, to the findings of forensics experts'" (qtd. in Messent 12). I should point out here, though, that Paretsky's private investigator, Warshawski has, on occasion, paid a private forensic analysis firm to check out crucial evidence she's obtained at crime scenes, and has also managed, with the approval of the victim's loved ones, to have second post-mortems carried out by private practitioners (Blacklist 228). So there are ways around these obstacles, fictionally at least. But, by and large, critics suggest that the private eye has been supplanted, in the area of 'realistic' crime fiction, by the police procedural.

The police procedural has assumed a much greater profile in crime fiction in recent years, to the extent that it threatens the existence of the private eye sub-genre, with Messent arguing that the change in emphasis away from the private investigator is "an acknowledgement of the fact that, in a contemporary world where the making visible of crime has come to depend more and more on sophisticated scientific technique and the ability to collate information quickly and on a large-scale and official basis, the private eye is increasingly irrelevant to, and necessarily blinkered in, this process" (11).

So, where does this leave the amateur sleuth in this hierarchy, regardless of success rates? Either at the bottom or nowhere, as Chandler so definitively and amusingly points out. In the 'real' world, by way of comparison, amateurs and private eyes, where they exist, have little or no access to the resources of police forces, by which I mean all levels of institutional policing. In Australia, for instance, this includes state police and the AFP (Australian Federal Police), as well as organisations such as ASIO (Australian Security Intelligence Organisation), ASIS (Australian Secret Intelligence Service), and the ONA (Office of National Assessments). These organisations liaise with defence force agencies as well, such as the DSD (Defence Signals Directorate), and the DIO (Defence Intelligence Organisation). The weight of sheer numbers, and of institutional authority and legislative prohibitions on unauthorised access to the information held, and the power of these agencies, ensures that the concept of the amateur investigator in particular, is a fictional one which developed during a period when organised policing was in its infancy. But, having acknowledged this, it is also the case that fiction has never let fact get in the way of a good story. Fact is a stepping-off point for fiction and, in murder fiction, strategies abound for overcoming and circumventing what the plethora of acronyms referred to above represent. An emphasis on characterisation is an increasingly significant factor in this regard; proximal investigators succeed as effective protagonists through an integration of real world demographic imperatives with sub-generic character conventions in order to fulfil the reader's horizon of expectations.

The reader's horizon of expectation allows for another kind of verisimilitude, and while the police procedural in various guises (plainclothes detectives, uniformed police, forensic investigators) has become very popular, not only in novels, but also on television, as the most 'realistic' type of crime story, texts featuring both the amateur and the private eye continue to achieve massive sales and unabating popularity. This other kind of verisimilitude, of which Miss Marple is a prime example, is intra-textual or internal, relating to the reality of the text and its consistency and believability. The popularity of amateur and private investigators would seem to indicate that the worlds these sub-genres offer continue to appeal to readers despite their contentious fit with current investigative and policing practices. These worlds demonstrate the expansion of the contemporary crime fiction scene and, while the amateurs and private eyes – these products of "romantic moonshine" – may not exist in the real world as murder solving sleuths, they do reflect the real world in terms of their demographics. Their lifestyles, their social networks, their familial situations, their political perspectives, in short, their sites of proximity, are based in late 20th- and early 21st-century realities; the same can be said for the characters in police procedurals. They are more than the investigations they carry out and this is one of the commonalities across these sub-genres, that is, the deepening and broadening of these primary roles, hence my decision to apply the term proximal investigator to them, regardless of their position on any formulaic-mimetic continuum of sleuths, and regardless of their adherence to extra- or intra-textual verisimilitude in relation to their crime-fighting roles.

The adoption of one descriptive term is reinforced by the occasional blurring of roles while operating within a particular category, such as the hard-boiled private eye sub-genre. Rawlins, for example, the proximal investigator in Mosley's series of novels set in Los Angeles from the late 1940s onwards, sidesteps the issue of amateur versus private eye by falling between the two, at least initially and, in so doing, establishes himself as a proximal investigator in a unique position to succeed. His milieu and his race are his assets as much as they are liabilities, and the Los Angeles landscape through which he moves is his salvation and his damnation. He begins his career in Devil in a Blue Dress as an investigator because he can move with impunity through areas of the city in South Central Los Angeles not open to white men like DeWitt Albright, who hires him to look for a woman, Daphne Monet. Daphne is accused of stealing a large sum of money from her wealthy, influential boyfriend who, for various reasons, doesn't want to involve the police. In a variation on Freda Adler's observation that "stripped of ethical rationalisations and philosophical pretensions, a crime is anything that a group in power chooses to prohibit" (155), Albright justifies his own and his employer's actions with the self-serving statement: "the law is made by the rich people so that the poor people can't get ahead. You don't want to get mixed up with the law and neither do I" (Mosley 27). For his part, Easy finds Albright repulsive, describing his handshake as "strong but slithery, like a snake coiling around my hand" (10), and admits to being afraid of him. But Easy adapts Albright's description of what he does for a living, a "'fella who does favors for friends, and for friends of friends'" (12), to describe himself in a similar fashion to his mentor, Odell, at the end of the novel, as someone who does "private investigations" for "people I know and people they know" (218). Easy can even pinpoint the period of time during his search, as he's looking for the mobster and hijacker, Frank Green, a pivotal figure in the story, when he becomes a detective:

> It was those two days more than any other time that made me a detective.
>
> I felt a secret glee when I went into a bar and ordered a beer with money someone else had paid me. I'd ask the bartender his name and talk about anything, but, really, behind my friendly talk, I was working to find something. Nobody knew what I was up to and that made me sort of invisible, people thought that they saw me but what they really saw was an illusion of me, something that wasn't real.
>
> I never got bored or frustrated. I wasn't even afraid of DeWitt Albright during those days. I felt, foolishly, safe from even his crazy violence. (134-35)

Initially, though, Easy is motivated to accept Albright's money because he's been laid off from his job (the sacking is due to his boss's racism) and needs money quickly to pay his mortgage: "that house meant more to me than any woman I ever knew. I loved her and I was jealous of her and if the bank sent the county marshal to take her from me I might have come at him with a rifle rather than to give her up" (19-20). While Easy's race and the precinct of the city he knows intimately are prominent sites of proximity as well as personal assets, at least some of the time, his extra-special attribute is what he calls the Voice. Like Smilla's feeling for snow, Easy's Voice constitutes a kind of sixth sense, a protective internal adviser which first appears when Easy is fighting in Normandy in World War Two. His two colleagues have been killed by a sniper who has Easy pinned down in a barn. The Voice, he explains:

> only comes to me at the worst times, when everything seems so bad that I want to take my car and drive it into a wall. Then this voice comes to me and gives me the best advice I ever get. The voice is hard. It never cares if I'm scared or in danger. It just looks at all the facts and tells me what I need to do.
>
> The voice told me to "get off yo' butt when the sun comes down an' kill that motherfucker. Kill him an' rip off his fuckin' face with yo' bayonet, man. You can't let him do that to you. Even if he lets you live you be scared the rest'a yo' life. Kill that motherfucker," he told me. And I did.
>
> The voice has no lust. He never told me to rape or steal. He just tells me how it is if I want to survive. Survive like a man.
>
> ... When the voice speaks, I listen. (104-06)

Easy's Voice has its genesis in sites of proximity that represent violence and death, and the threat of violence and death for the protagonist. Smilla's feeling for snow is also associated with violence and death, and the threat towards her and her loved ones of violence and death. They are qualities that propel the protagonists to act in particular ways that differentiate them from everyone else and paradoxically, in the course of the narratives, they act as endangering factors, too. It is Easy's Voice that encourages him to act courageously in the face of death, to take on challenges he would otherwise avoid, in order to secure his future, his home, and the potential for one day having a family life. It is Smilla's feeling for snow that ensures her involvement in solving the mystery of Isaiah's death, despite her desire for a life empty of responsibilities and the complications that relationships inevitably bring with them. Ultimately, neither Easy nor Smilla can resist the call to adventure, to take on the hero's journey, the reward at the end of which is twofold, reflecting their roles as proximal investigators and as individuals with histories and futures. They solve the crimes, and reinforce the notion of a purposeful existence in their respective worlds (even with Smilla's conclusion that "you can't win against the ice" [410] – she does, after all, have a better chance than most of success), valuable outcomes for series characters in particular.

In a similar vein, the main character in Mankell's police procedural series, Detective Inspector Kurt Wallander, operating out of the town of Ystad on the southern coast of Sweden, defines himself by both his life as a policeman: "he was a policeman to the core" (Faceless 144), and his family and personal relationships. In Faceless Killers, the first in the Wallander series, the investigator's personal life and problems have the potential to overwhelm his career. He is soon to be divorced from his wife, Mona ("'If I hadn't left you, I would have died,' she said" [141]), and estranged from his daughter, Linda, after she attempted suicide several years before. He endures a hostile relationship with his father, who never wanted him to become a policeman but has never explained why, and who appears to be developing dementia. The close relationship he once enjoyed with his sister, Kristina, has deteriorated through neglect, and his neglect of his health since his separation from his wife has resulted in weight gain, poor diet, excessive drinking (he endangers his career when he is picked up by two uniformed officers for drink driving), and sleep disturbances. Early in the investigation into the brutal murders of an elderly couple at their farmhouse, he castigates himself:

> On the way to the press conference he went to the men's room and looked in the mirror. He saw that he needed a haircut. His brown hair was sticking out round his ears. And he ought to lose some weight too. In the three months since his wife had left him, he had put on seven kilos. In his apathetic loneliness he had eaten nothing but takeaways and pizza, greasy hamburgers and pastries.
>
> "You flabby piece of shit," he said out loud. "Do you really want to look like a pitiful old man?"
>
> He made a decision to change his eating habits at once. If it would help him lose weight, he might even consider taking up smoking again. He wondered why almost every policeman was divorced. Why their wives left them. Sometimes, when he read a crime novel, he discovered with a sigh that things were just as bad in fiction. Policemen were divorced. That's all there was to it. (17)

But along with self-criticism (reflecting the self-referentiality of crime fiction), there is also self-belief, and a belief in his career as a vocation. His inner voice is nothing like Rawlins's assertive provocateur. It doesn't so much offer forceful exhortations as a hopeful but fatalistic mantra based in fear and a great respect for his mortality, even as he ignores to a large extent his basic physical and psychological needs. Early in his career, Wallander was close to death after being stabbed by a drunk he was trying to arrest. The knife was millimetres from his heart and an untimely death at 23, and he was made "suddenly profoundly aware of what it meant to be a policeman" (9). After this experience, he adopted what he calls an incantation: "a time to live and a time to die," which he regards as his way of "fending off the memories" (9). He invokes his incantation several times throughout the narrative, as he reflects on his own brushes with death, and on the situation of others such as his friend and colleague, Rydberg, who is dying of cancer. Wallander's inner voice is representative of an acquiescence to the frequently random nature of death, and it is also a respectful acknowledgement of his own mortality and his acceptance of his decision to remain a detective regardless of the risks. He was born to be a policeman – the job is his custom fit life, despite its effects on his health and happiness – and he has no intention of changing his fate, whatever it might be. Like Jaspersen and Rawlins, he continues to put himself at risk, placing himself in harm's way throughout the narrative in pursuit of the truth, engaging with the commonest site of proximity of all for the proximal investigator: death.

In Faceless Killers, this is a site surrounded and suffused by other sites of proximity including the politics of immigration, racism, and discrimination against refugees who have settled in Sweden and who are perceived to be disruptive, contrary influences on the social order. Mankell has indicated that his crime novels are a way of commenting on issues of significance: "'You hold a mirror to crime to see what's happening in society. I could never write a crime story just for the sake of it, because I always want to talk about certain things in society'" (qtd. in Thomson np). Faceless Killers was written when Mankell returned to Sweden after living in Mozambique for two years, and became aware of the increasing incidence of crimes of violence against immigrants by neo-fascist groups. His decision to write a crime story, and specifically a police procedural, was based in the recognition of racism as a crime and the logic of connecting the genre with the issue. In addition, Mankell connects with other significant sites of proximity, including those that engage with notions of personal responsibility and the dynamics of familial relationships that are reflective of contemporary Western societies. Wallander's character blends his fears for his own future as a lonely, divorced man, with his proximal investigator's knowledge – the superior knowledge of the insider – and fear, of a changing society in which violence figures more prominently. And it is frequently unexplainable violence, as evidenced by the refusal, or inability, of the murderers of the helpless elderly victim, Maria Lövgren, to tell Wallander why they put a noose around her neck: "Neither man would confess to that insane violence" (278). For Wallander, it is evidence of what he calls "the new era, which demanded a different kind of policeman. We're living in the age of the noose, he thought. Fear will be on the rise" (280). Yet he remains essentially a man who is more than his vocation, more than a police investigator, though also irrevocably shaped by his job – it is the breath of life for him – who nonetheless seeks respite in unconsciousness: "He forced himself to push these thoughts aside and sought out the black woman of his dreams. The investigation was over. Now he could finally get some rest" (280), at least until the next crime occurs and offers its variety of sites of proximity for exploration.

The use of crime fiction sub-genres to engage in an overt way with sites of personal, social, and political proximity, as in the Wallander stories, is pervasive in contemporary crime narratives. Evolving from its beginnings as "an expression of conservative, bourgeois, ethnocentric Anglo-American values" (Dellamater and Prigozy 9), crime fiction, according to Cawelti, has become "a genre in which writers explore new social values and definitions and push against the traditional boundaries of gender and race to play imaginatively with new kinds of social character and human relations" (8). Paretsky created Warshawski partly to present a fictional counterbalance to the prevailing images of women in hard-boiled detective stories from the 1930s to the 1970s as either "'sexually active and therefore instantly identifiable as evil, or sexually chaste, in which case they could not act at all'" (qtd. in Reynolds 140). As one of the earlier representatives of second-wave feminist crime writing, along with Carolyn Heilbrun (writing as Amanda Cross), Marcia Muller, and Grafton, Paretsky's novels show, according to Walton and Jones, "a nostalgia for the idealistic social action of the 1960s and early 1970s, when the women's movement (and activism more generally) seemed to hold so much promise for changing both society as a whole and individual lives" (34).

It is from this background that Warshawski's custom fit quality as a proximal investigator emerges, and develops over the course of the series. This quality, rather than a specific skill such as Jaspersen's feeling for snow, or a clear sixth-sense Voice, as with Rawlins, or the mantra Wallander intones, is Warshawski's idealism. Her idealism is a state of mind and a methodology she applies to her vocation as a private eye, but it is grounded in a realist's view of the world. Because of its more diffuse nature, this character and her special quality require a fuller discussion than those characters discussed above, whose unique attributes are more clearly delineated.

As with other proximal investigators, Warshawski's idealism is both a protective and an endangering quality, which also acts as a kind of weapon with assertive/offensive and defensive elements. Again and again, in successive novels, Warshawski is at the point of defeat, death, of imminent career suicide at the hands of powerful and seemingly overwhelming forces and, repeatedly, she succeeds despite every odd being against her, thus embodying the notion of the hero on a quest more emphatically than Jaspersen, Rawlins, or Wallander. Her idealism is action-based, and it also infuses the narrative through her approach to her proximal investigations. Besides bestowing an ability to recover spectacularly from blows to the head and elsewhere, from kidnapping, pistol-whipping, and firebombing – her strength truly is 'as the strength of ten' – Warshawski's eternal flame of idealism moves with her and is expressed through her truth-seeking missions, missions which exemplify her desire to secure justice, particularly for the vulnerable, the helpless, and the exploited.

Although her fights are against insurance corporations (Indemnity Only), big business (Fire Sale), and government institutions, including the prison system (Hard Time) and federal agencies (Blacklist), Warshawski's idealism isn't abstract or necessarily attached to an absolutist perspective, but focusses on individuals and the complexities of their relationships with each other and with their social, political and economic milieus. As Maureen Reddy observes of feminist crime writers, "there is no single, universal truth … rather, truth is always relative, dependent on perspective and on circumstances" (176). As Paretsky presents her, Warshawski's reasons for becoming involved in cases are usually personal: a friend or family member needs help, which supports Reddy's assertion that feminist detectives most commonly take on investigations because they have a personal stake of some kind in them (176). Their motivation is seldom money, power, or control, influential factors that are frequently sources of the crimes they investigate, but rather a recognition that individuals have rights that must be protected and where they have been removed or are threatened or absent, must be restored.

Paretsky notes that Warshawski, born in the 1950s, is closely connected with the Civil Rights and anti-Vietnam war movements, and with second-wave feminism ("Interview" np), as is Paretsky herself, once again confirming the relatively high levels of identification among female authors with the attitudes and qualities of their fictional protagonists (DellaCava and Engel xi). Human rights generally – an idealist's optimal site of proximity – but particularly in relation to their disregard and corruption by large institutions, including corporations and government, emerge as a powerful motivator for Warshawski in taking on cases. Further, the reader is consistently reminded of Warshawski's background as the daughter of working-class parents (her father was a police officer and her mother a refugee from Fascist Italy) from the wrong side of the tracks, in one of Chicago's poorer neighborhoods (South Chicago). Through her own hard labour and diligence, and supported by an athletics scholarship (elaborated on in Fire Sale), she earned a law degree, but turned her back on working for institutions in favour of investigating them as a private eye and independent agent, thus giving a voice to those who find themselves silenced in the face of collective power and malevolent influence. As an "eager young lawyer" for the Public Defender, as she explains to Ralph Devereux in the first Warshawski novel, *Indemnity Only*, she came to see herself as essentially maintaining the status quo in the face of a never-ending tide of hapless clients:

> "The setup is pretty corrupt – you're never arguing for justice, always on points of law. I wanted to get out of it, but I still wanted to do something that would make me feel that I was working on my concept of justice, not legal point-scoring. I resigned from the Public Defender's office, and was wondering what to do next, when a girl came to me and asked me to clear her brother of a robbery charge. He looked hopelessly guilty – it was a charge of stealing video equipment from a big corporate studio, and he had access, opportunity, and so on, but I took the case on and I discovered he was innocent by finding out who the guilty person really was." (156)

This realist's idealism, rooted in the site of proximity that is human rights, is represented in Blacklist, which was published in 2003, two years after the terrorist attacks on the World Trade Centre. Blacklist's plot deals with changes in the American justice system brought about by the United States' Government's Patriot Act and the concomitant rise in anxiety about, and fear of terrorism following the Trade Centre attacks. These fears included who in the population might be a potential terrorist, an actual terrorist, or be likely to aid or harbour a potential or actual terrorist, a person whose "race, creed or place of national origin" the authorities "don't like" (215), as Warshawski succinctly summarises. She talks to her neighbour and de facto father figure, Sal Contreras, when a Federal agent pursues her to her apartment after she's helped to hide with a friend a suspected terrorist named Benji Sadawi. Sadawi is an Egyptian immigrant whose visa has expired, and Warshawski explains: "'According to that walking manual in the tan overcoat, they can go to any home in America, claim the owner is concealing Osama bin Laden, and enter without a warrant. And if you object, they bust down the door'" (239). The plot also draws parallels – via another sub-plot relating to blackmail and Communist affiliations in the upper echelons of Chicago society – with the McCarthy era of the 1950s, when Cold War anti-Communist hysteria in America was exemplified and fuelled by the House Un-American Activities Committee, chaired by Republican Senator Joseph McCarthy. Paretsky, a child of the 1950s like Warshawski has, in a number of essays and interviews, expressed her fears and concerns about the removal, by the Patriot Act, of protections taken for granted by citizens, such as rights to privacy and freedom of speech without fear of arrest or of being silenced by legislative intimidation. Paretsky refers to "friends and family whose lives McCarthy ... made miserable" ("Literary" np) and to her own childhood in a conservative mid-Western town (Lawrence, Kansas) in which protecting the town "against Communism was an obsession" ("Truth" np). In Blacklist, Warshawski, the proximal investigator with her custom fit quality of idealism, shares her creator's fears and ideological perspective: "'The McCarthy and HUAC blacklists shattered lives. People never worked again, or never worked well …. Some committed suicide. Many went to prison, only for their beliefs, not for anything they'd done'" (409). The observations of friends like Lottie Herschel, her de facto mother figure, show that Warshawski is unlikely to be dissuaded from a course of action she believes to be just. After Warshawski explains that she has hidden Benji Sadawi with Father

Lou at St Remigio's church and monastery, Lottie sums up her friend's approach to every investigation:

> "I hope for everyone's sake you're right about this, Victoria. I'm worried about, oh, everything, but also your own safety. You could get badly hurt yourself, you know. Not even necessarily by this boy, but by some gun-happy policeman like the ones who shot the Bayard child. Is this Egyptian boy's health and safety really worth the risk to your own life?" Her mouth twisted in an ironic smile. "Why am I even asking that question? You're like your own dogs – once you have a bone in your teeth, you won't let it go." (305-06)

Warshawski's idealism, founded in a realist's perspective, and one of the major reasons why she constantly picks up such 'bones,' is revealed more clearly when she confronts Renee Bayard, the woman who murdered both the investigative journalist Marcus Whitby, to protect her husband's reputation – the crime that drew Warshawski into the investigation – and the eyewitness to Whitby's murder, the innocent non-terrorist, Benji Sadawi. Renee dismisses Warshawski's suggestion that Renee's granddaughter, Catherine, who protected Benji initially, won't want to remain with her now that she knows the truth, telling Warshawski that, since she has no children and no home life, she is no judge of family relationships. "I thought of my mother's fierce love for me," she reflects, "and my father's more level affection; the price they demanded in return was not adoration, nor achievement, but integrity. I could not lie or cheat to avoid trouble" (393).

*

The political commentary in Blacklist, based as it is in extraordinary real-life events and their equally extraordinary ongoing consequences, is perhaps more heavy-handed, or didactic, than that engaged with by Mosley in Devil in a Blue Dress, Høeg in Miss Smilla's Feeling for Snow, or Mankell in Faceless Killers, but the aims are similar: to interweave murder plots, or the site of proximity that is death, with sites of proximity that reinforce crime fiction's capacity to engage with 'new social values and definitions' as part of its hybrid, evolutionary nature. They offer more or less fully-realised protagonists to negotiate the narrative, investigators capable of engaging with sites of proximity that reflect contemporary social, political, gender, race, economic, and other issues.

In this chapter, I have proposed a new name for the variety of investigators that populate these and other murder texts: the proximal investigator. I have argued that removing the titles of private eye, police officer, amateur sleuth, and so on, and applying the term proximal investigator, facilitates a means of approaching these characters without the biases inherent in, and assumptions attached to such titles, thereby enabling a clearer view of their roles and their strategic connections to particular sites of proximity. I have also argued that, since Poe's depiction of Dupin, investigators have been portrayed with the aim of offering a 'same but different' reading experience, which promotes the notion of a custom fit text. This notion has expanded to incorporate an almost limitless variety of offerings of such texts in contemporary crime fiction. Part of the custom fit is a proximal investigator who possesses special attributes that distinguish this investigator from all the others across the range of sub-genres that make up murder texts. The texts in which they appear are published and promoted on the basis of these unique characters whose private lives beyond and apart from investigations are detailed as never before. But it also essential to remind ourselves that the existence of the proximal investigator in murder fiction, no matter how unusual or successful, is wholly dependent on the victims, those unfortunate characters whose destiny it is to become corpses of convenience. I explore their role in murder fiction texts, and the site of proximity that is death, in the next chapter.

CHAPTER THREE

Death and the Family: Two Key Sites of Criminal and Creative Proximity

When you're writing a kind of instinct comes into play. What you're going to write is already there in the darkness. It's as if writing were something outside you, in a tangle of tenses between writing and having written, having written and having to go on writing; between knowing and not knowing what it's all about; starting from complete meaning, being submerged by it, and ending up in meaninglessness. The image of a black block in the middle of the world isn't far out.
Marguerite Duras, Practicalities 25

One can apply the notion of sites of proximity in relation to the writer in the same way David Malouf suggests that writers return again and again in their work to a relatively small number of subjects ("Poetry"). In writing my novel, "Thicker Than Water," I was able to return to two of these subjects, or key sites of creative proximity for me and, I think, for countless writers, that are also essential to the success of investigator-based murder texts. These sites are death, represented in murder texts by the corpse of convenience, and the family which, in murder texts, comprises the suspects in the novel; in a collective sense I refer to them as the family of circumstance. Duras' eloquent description of writing also alludes to the idea of writers returning to a few select subjects of deepest interest when she suggests that the work is already there, the subjects are awaiting one's return. Their ever-presence "in the darkness" is by no means a guarantee of understanding them, but rather underlines the very reason for the return. We seek to understand our few subjects of interest, our key sites of creative proximity, in every text we write. They will always be there for us to explore, never quite understood, and never quite finished with. In murder novels, representations of death and the family are especially critical contributors to the custom fit text.

When researching and writing "Thicker Than Water," I was aware of the influence on my thinking and writing of a range of crime fiction sub-genres and of particular writers' approaches to the custom fit through the presentation and disposition of the corpse of convenience and the family of circumstance. While one basic aim of crime fiction, if not its primary reason for existing, is to operate as a form of entertainment, crime fiction also poses legitimate questions about the nature of our society and its relationships with subjects like death and notions of the family. In this chapter, I examine some perspectives on the place of death in contemporary Western society and its relationship with murder fiction, before considering examples of the corpse of convenience in texts representing different sub-genres of investigator-based murder fiction. These sub-genres suggest that death, while it remains essentially unknowable, is both observable and measurable, the latter from the perspective of the levels of emotional involvement of the reader, the proximal investigator, and other members of the family of circumstance. After this, I offer a discussion of the family of circumstance.

DEATH AND THE UNPREDICTABLE SUSPENSE OF CERTAINTY

It has been said that 'nobody cares about the corpse.' This is bunk. It is throwing away a valuable element. It is like saying the murder of your aunt means no more to you than the murder of an unknown man in an unknown part of a city you never visited.

Raymond Chandler, Notebooks 38

The twentieth century, as Andrew Taylor points out, was the most violent on record, though this may owe more to our ability to destroy huge numbers of the world's human population (which is higher than at any other time in history) with advanced weaponry and technology, than to any changes in levels of hostility or aggression. Nonetheless, we are surrounded by death and images of death because of our ready access to media such as television and the Internet, and by the intrusiveness of these media in our lives. But real life images and stories are frequently presented in ways that distance us as observers and readers. They are structured and packaged, edited and polished to the point where, in a sense, they meet fiction coming from the opposite direction, and often manage to integrate with it. Anyone who has experienced a news story unfolding behind the scenes is likely to be aware that the narrative that is read in a television news program, or which appears in a newspaper, offers a necessarily selective perspective, relying on the exaggeration of some elements and the suppression of others, to the extent that inaccuracies develop and embed themselves in the narrative. As with a fictional narrative, no news report presents – nor would it be possible to do so – every detail of the original, chronological sequence of events, the absent story (although, from an ethical standpoint, of course, the integrity of the facts, as far as they are known, should be respected, but unreliable narration is by no means the exclusive preserve of fiction writers). (Note 10: When I created the character Ari

Babitsky, I researched the murders by Palestinian Liberation Organi-sation (PLO) terrorists of Israeli athletes during the 1972 Munich Olympics. I discovered, not surprisingly, that a number of non-fiction texts and television documentaries differ, sometimes quite markedly, in their depictions, among other elements, of the se-quences of events, the Israeli government's consequent actions, and the motivations of Mossad agents appointed to find and execute those involved in the Munich murders. Steven Spielberg's film, *Munich*, has been endorsed by some critics and analysts for its accuracy and dismissed by others for its errors and misrepresentations). Christine Jackson argues that the media "show us images of real murders made fake on the news and staged murders made real on the shows. Mystery reading gains ascendancy by riding this exploita-tion" (9). From the other end of the non-fiction-to-fiction scale, like much news reporting, crime fiction is a genre that engages and inte-grates very successfully with contemporary issues and offers narra-tives that both comfort and confront by serving up a carefully restructured, controlled realism from which, depending on the sub-genre, readers may derive any given depth of vicarious thrills, anxie-ties and fears. One of the overriding narratives that crime fiction, or more specifically, murder fiction offers, and one of the subjects that provokes the most anxiety, fear and sense of thrill, is death.

Death, represented by murder, is the indispensable site of prox-imity in investigator-based murder novels, and murder, as discussed in chapter one, is the crime of choice in contemporary crime fiction. Death, paradoxically, breathes life into the character of the proximal investigator in that there is no reason for these protagonists to exist otherwise, and the event of death establishes very clearly the essence of the dual narrative of the absent crime (the action or story as it occurs in real time) and the present investigation (the discourse that is the plot and the reconstruction of the story). The ways in which this site – through the character of the victim – is connected to the investigator and other sites of proximity, contribute to creating a custom fit reading experience. This site of proximity, death, also helps to identify what kind of murder novel we are reading, from the clue-puzzle cosy, to the police procedural, to the most graphic of the serial killer sub-genre. The characters which represent death in any of these texts are always victims of sudden violence. Murder: the unlawful taking of a life, can be nothing but violent and sudden by definition, and these murder victims are always – no matter what the sub-genre, and no matter what their relationships with a text's other characters, including the murderer – corpses of convenience.

But these corpses of convenience are also corpses of inconvenience. By their silent presence, they attest to our fears, they demand a reaction, and they demand more than glancing attention. In her essay, "Negotiating with the Dead," Atwood considers what the dead may want from the living. After considering the ways in which different cultures honour and acknowledge the dead – through days of commemoration (Remembrance Day, All Souls Day), ceremonies involving offerings of food (Mexico's Day of the Dead) – she suggests that the dead want to be remembered, but that they may also want revenge for real or perceived sins against them (Banquo's ghost in Macbeth, for instance). "If we could sum up what all of them want, in one word – a word that encompasses life, sacrifice, food, and death – that word would be 'blood'" (147). The dead want to live again in some form.

The dead in crime fiction fulfil at least two important roles in their desire to live again: they are the plot points on which the narrative turns (a crime occurs and attempts are made to solve it [Porter 5]), and both the story's investigator and the reader may develop emotional attachments to them, desirous of revenge on their behalf. The absent dead are made present and live again, in a manner of speaking, through the process of investigation. The pursuit of justice for the absent victim, who becomes familiar through the reconstruction of events leading to the crime, and the crime itself, may also allow the victim to become, depending on how their absent life is represented, an object of affection, and a source of both distress and comfort.

Part of the reading experience of crime fiction, and of murder novels, fulfilling the reader's horizon of expectations, is the reinforcement, in the face of mortal danger, of notions of comfort and safety. This comfort and safety appears in the form of what I call the unpredictable suspense of certainty in fictional worlds where order is initially disrupted through a criminal act; in this discussion, the act of murder. We read these texts to experience "moments of intense excitement and interest" (Cawelti 15) in their representations of "changing objects of popular anxiety" (Porter 127), understanding, simultaneously, that the advent of chaos contains within it a guarantee of order restored, of the return of comfort and safety. Oates puts it neatly: "The promise of the mystery-detective novel is that its beginning, its very opening statement, is simultaneously its ending, the terror of ambiguity resolved" (35). Such promises hold no water in the real world where, although one can identify recurring cycles of order followed by chaos and then a return to a new kind of order, albeit different from the original state of equilibrium, there is no certainty. There is unpredictability and suspense, routine and order, and the illusion of control, if one doesn't enquire too deeply or press too hard. There is no certainty, but rather there are greater or lesser degress of probability which predict that, much of the time, things will unfold more or less according to expectations. Escapist literature, as Cawelti points out, serves the dual purpose of providing, for the reader who lives in a relatively safe and orderly country, the promise of vicarious thrills, danger, suspense, and life-threatening incidents, via our favourite protagonists and assorted characters, in the safety net of conventions and rules, and with the structural familiarity of the crime text, the ending prophesied at the beginning (14-17). It is through this frame of manufactured suspense and fear, tempered by ultimate narrative certainty (and safety) that we view the site of proximity that is death, and the character who is, or who becomes the corpse of convenience, a character who we may come to know very well in the course of the narrative.

Jackson suggests that in "death-repressed" (9) Western cultures "the detective novel perpetrates a great lie – that death is knowable" (4), and I agree that, from a particular perspective, this is exactly what the detective novel is designed to do as part of its comfort effect. This sort of novel suggests that death is knowable as part of its contract with the reader who is searching for an escape from the self-knowledge of their own mortality and the uncertainty of when death may occur in a world of random fate. How does it do this? One way is that the proximal investigator embodies the "lie" of knowability on behalf both of the reader and the corpse of convenience, acting as the protective, filtering agent who reveals why the murder occurred and who is responsible, with the aim of bringing about the neat combination outcome of understanding and justice, leading to closure. In addition, the proximal investigator re-animates the corpse of convenience through the work of gumshoeing, paying the victim the respect of dedicated inquiry. Through this inquiry, we acquire different bodies of knowledge about the corpse of convenience and about death, depending on the sub-genre – each one offering a variety of control mechanisms – and the more knowledge we have, the greater our level of control. More accurately, perhaps, it is our perception that control is possible, so that perception becomes reality. In this scenario, control of knowledge equals control of death and, if we can control and contain death, perhaps we can somehow come to understand more about it in a way that wasn't possible before. A question that arises is, what knowledge does the site of proximity that is death, represented by the corpse of convenience, offer that contributes to perpetrating, and perpetuating the lie of knowability?

In the case of the serial killer text, for example, close attention is paid to a forensic deconstruction, and re-construction, of the victims in order to understand the standard questions of how, where, and when the victim died, and by what means, the answers to which enquiries, if accurately uncovered and integrated, may lead (but not always) to why the murder occurred and who did it, a body of knowledge that profiles both perpetrator and corpse of convenience and, to an extent, the menacing and dangerous society they inhabit. While a range of factors is considered, the greatest primary, and primal effects in texts such as those written by Cornwell are derived from the graphic nature of the scene of the crime and disposition of the corpse, followed by the dissection of the corpse at autopsy by, in this case, Medical Examiner Scarpetta.

In Post-Mortem, the first Scarpetta novel, pubished in 1990, the opening scenes initially depict Scarpetta as a lone figure, our trustworthy proximal investigator, our eyes, as it were, awakened from sleep and a dream – is it? – of a malevolent presence watching and waiting for her outside the current safety zone of her home (breached by the killer during the climax), establishing a de-centred world of instability with as-yet unspecified threats and potential chaos waiting for release:

> I saw a white face beyond the rain-streaked glass, a face formless and inhuman like the faces of misshapen dolls made of nylon hose. My bedroom window was dark when suddenly the face was there, an evil intelligence looking in.
>
> I woke up and stared blindly into the dark. (3)

Scarpetta's arousal from sleep and her entry into another work day, where her position as a member of a law and order collective becomes apparent, can be seen as a metaphor for the entire series, in which the thin blue line of the various American policing agencies, including the local police and the Federal Bureau of Investigation (FBI), stages a never-ending, frequently violent and, for the most part, vigilant war against the ubiquitous forces of evil, personified in the Scarpetta novels as psychopathic serial killers.

When she goes out into the already menacing night, Scarpetta confronts a horrible crime scene, the product of the latest homicide by a murderer who we learn has already struck several times. We are confronted with graphic details of how this victim was murdered:

> One cord bound her wrists, which were pinioned at the small of her back. The other cord was tied in a diabolically creative pattern also consistent with the first three cases. Looped once around her neck, it was threaded behind her through the cord around her wrists and tightly lashed around her ankles. As long as her knees were bent, the loop around her neck remained loose. When she straightened

> her legs, either in a reflex to pain or because of the assail-
> ant's weight on top of her, the ligature around her neck
> tightened like a noose.
>
> Death by asphyxiation takes only several minutes.
> That's a very long time when every cell in your body is
> screaming for air. (14)

This description of the mechanics of tortuous suffocation is followed by its visually obvious effects on the victim's body: "Her face
was grotesque, swollen beyond recognition and a dark bluish purple
from the suffusion of blood caused by the tight ligature around her
neck. Bloody fluid had leaked from her nose and mouth, staining the
sheet" (15). Later, when Scarpetta conducts the autopsy, we are again
assaulted with the physiological evidence of human frailty and suf-
fering, and of the magnitude of the killer's cruelty and psychopathy:
"Three ribs in a row on the left side were fractured, as were four of
her fingers. There were fibers inside her mouth, mostly on her
tongue, suggesting that at some point she was gagged to prevent her
from screaming" (36).

This corpse of convenience, through the intervention of the
proximal investigator, Scarpetta, connects us to the unspeakable, to
the Other in the form of the serial killer who is seen, in these pre-
liminary circumstances of ignorance, as inhuman. Later, he is revealed as all-too-human, at least in appearance, although the absence
(from Scarpetta's perspective) of a quality (a soul) invisible to the
human eye, but which may be essential to a compassionate humani-
ty, ensures his exclusion from any kindly consideration by the reader: "He was just a pasty-faced boy with dirty-blond hair. His
mustache was nothing more than a dirty fuzz. I would never forget

those eyes. They were windows through which I saw no soul. They were empty windows opening onto a darkness" (388).

There is a repetition here of negative concepts such as "darkness," "evil," "evil intelligence," and "inhuman." The images of windows at the beginning and end of the novel suggest portals between good and bad worlds, between light and dark, and the corruption and degradation of colours adds to the differentiation: the killer is "pasty-faced," has "dirty-blond" hair, and "a dirty fuzz" for a moustache. The apparent soullessness of Post-Mortem's killer is reminiscent of Poe's description of the man of the crowd as possessing the face of a "fiend." A fiend, apart from being an "enemy" or "foe," is also defined as "an evil spirit; a demon, a devil or diabolical being …. A person of superhuman wickedness; especially cruelty or malignity …. A monster, the personification of a baleful or destructive influence" (New 1: 943). Although the man of the crowd has committed no crime that Poe's narrator can detect, he somehow understands that he is observing "the type and the genius of deep crime," an unknowable force and one that, unlike Scarpetta and her team, he is glad to leave to his own devices, unwilling to become a victim of crime himself and welcoming the relative safety of the dawn light.

In Scarpetta's world, the corpse of convenience is a completely hapless victim of a modern "genius of deep crime" and dark forces, as innocent as a baby in her ignorance of the particular qualitites that attract the "diabolically creative" efforts of the "demonic" murderer. Scarpetta herself briefly embodies the position of the helpless victim at the beginning of Post-Mortem, waking from sleep, vulnerable, and staring "blindly into the dark." Unlike the other victims, Scarpetta has the skills and support network to investigate, pursue and, ultimately, capture the fiend, who is knowable from his prior actions, but also in the sense that he becomes controllable through incarceration or by being killed as he is, in this case, by Scarpetta's protector, police detective Pete Marino. But discovering who the murderer is, and being able to delineate a detailed profile of the causes and effects of his actions and obsession with killing doesn't bring us any closer to knowing death. It does, however, offer the comforting knowledge that established legal and investigative structures and their representatives, in the form of Scarpetta and her team, can restore order and banish chaos, for a short time at least, before the Other makes further, inevitable assaults on society's fragile equilibrium.

Cornwell demonstrates in her novels that death is about appearances. In other words, death is observable in minute detail through the corpse of convenience. The illusion of the knowability of death is given strength through graphic forensic evidence of mortality, evidence which typically and eventually answers the questions how, when, where, what, who and, in a qualified way, why. The question of why is surrounded by qualification in the serial killer text especially, because of unanswered questions (the subject of continuing research by scientists and law enforcement agencies among others) regarding the nature of psychopathy, sociopathy, and serial murderers. In other sub-genres, such as the amateur or private investigator, we may also occasionally encounter psychopaths who are mentally unbalanced sexual sadists, but the motivations for the actions of the bulk of murderers in these texts are usually less encouraging of speculation about demonic soullessness or the more pedestrian neurological damage or disorder, in favour of an emphasis on arguably a more immediately understandable economic or romantic soullessness. The greedy, the thwarted, and the spurned are dominant figures in these texts, and the corpse of convenience, ever-flexible, may be a direct target, or simply a victim of circumstance and similarly as hapless, therefore, as a serial killer's victim.

In Mosley's Devil in a Blue Dress, for example, the corpse of convenience performs a variety of roles including direct target and victim of circumstance, and is also representative and reflective of a way of life in a particular sub-culture. When proximal investigator, Rawlins, explains why he left Texas, he describes a society in which death is prevalent and life is literally cheap: "Back in Texas, in Fifth Ward, Houston, men would kill over a dime wager or a rash word" (40). The victims may be ignorant of the danger they were in because they weren't aware of it due either to their relative innocence or their lack of sense: "it was always the evil ones that would kill the good or the stupid" (40). But in Los Angeles, where Easy is drawn into a situation in which a number of people are killed because of stolen money and blackmail, things aren't very different. Easy realises that DeWitt Albright, the man who engages him to find Daphne Monet, who is both thief (she steals $30,000 from her white, wealthy ex-boyfriend) and blackmail victim (a number of people know that she is African-American and not white as she pretends), regards the taking of a life as a task with no pangs of conscience, sense of guilt, or responsibility attached to it. As he tells Easy: "'the only thing you have to remember, Easy ... is that some of us can kill with no more trouble than drinking a glass of bourbon.' He downed the shot and smiled" (30). For Albright, it is a question of business and potential profit. The murders that occur in Devil in a Blue Dress, along with the corpses of convenience that result, enable us to measure the perceived value of a life primarily in economic terms, in the violent and racist milieu of Los Angeles in the late 1940s. We see the lives of these characters from points of view that reinforce the sense of a dystopic vision, tempered only by Easy's hope (against hope) for a better life, represented tangibly by his house, a symbol of potential love in the form of marriage and a family, and a zone of stability and safety, all of which hangs on Easy's contract with the questionable Albright, and his ability to stay alive with the help of his Voice.

It appears clear that there are psychopaths among the characters Easy encounters, including Albright and Easy's 'friend,' Raymond 'Mouse' Alexander. Mouse, some of whose previous murders are the reason Easy left Houston, saves Easy's life merely because of his reputation as a cold-blooded killer when Easy is threatened by another killer, the gangster, Frank Green: "'I tell you what, Frank. You put down that knife right there on the couch an' I let you live. You don't an' you dead. I ain't gonna count or no bullshit like that now. Just one minute and I'm'a shoot'" (154). While Frank accedes to Mouse's request, understanding clearly that Mouse will kill him if he doesn't, the emphasis in this novel is on economic, status-related, and romantic motivations for killing and being killed rather than deeper psychoanalyses of individual personalities. The corpses of convenience in this milieu are, in a sense, markers – as are the victims in Cornwell's novels – of these motivations and others. Daphne Monet, for example, describes to Easy how she killed Matthew Teran, a paedophile and the man who was blackmailing her: "'I pulled the trigger, he died. But he killed himself really. I went to him, to ask him to leave me alone. I offered him all my money but he just laughed. He had his hands in that little boy's drawers and he laughed.' Daphne snorted. I don't know if it was a laugh or a sound of disgust. 'And so I killed him'" (207). But corpses of convenience like Teran, as well as marking or representing the motivations of others such as Daphne to end the blackmail, can become, in death, motivators in themselves. They are already automatic motivators for the proximal investigators but, beyond this, Daphne, for instance, as a result of Teran's death, and motivated because of this either by a sense of compassion or fear of exposure, takes the little boy to her home and later asks Easy to care for him. The boy becomes an integral member of Easy's family in later novels in Mosley's Rawlins series.

Another illustration of this dual purpose of the corpse of convenience as both a marker of others' motivations and as a motivator itself, involves Daphne's ex-boyfriend, Richard McGee, and the bouncer, Junior Fornay, who works at an illegal nightclub called John's, where Easy goes to search for Daphne Monet. Fornay, according to Easy, is "a filthy man who didn't give a damn about anything" (35), and he'd tried to murder Easy some years earlier until Mouse stepped in and saved him. In Devil in a Blue Dress, Fornay murders McGee (who is also a seller of children to paedophiles), a man Easy first notices when he visits John's place. As a corpse of convenience, McGee initially signifies others' motivations in the form of Fornay's greed and fear, and he then becomes a motivator for Easy to save himself from being charged with murder. Before his fatal encounter with Fornay, McGee stands out because he is white, he wears an expensive suit, and is also very drunk. He has come to the nightclub in search of Daphne and been ejected. Junior's aunt, Hattie Parsons, who runs the shop in front of the club and acts as a kind of lookout, tells Easy she'll get Junior to "sweep 'im up" (32) if he refuses to leave the area. Later, when Easy has located Daphne and they travel together to McGee's home in Laurel Canyon, they discover his body in the bedroom. This is one of only two relatively graphically described murder scenes in the novel. Five of six other murders that occur during the course of the narrative, those of Howard Green, Coretta James, Matthew Teran, Frank Green, and DeWitt Albright, are briefly reported by others to have occurred. The sixth, Mouse's murder of Joppy Shag, who in his turn has killed Howard Green and Coretta James, is witnessed by Easy when Mouse shoots Joppy in the groin and then in the eye. Easy concludes that Mouse did it for the money and also because he could: "Joppy had been my friend but I'd seen many men die and I cared for Coretta too" (206). Easy's comment that he cared for Coretta helps him to justify not intervening with Mouse to save Joppy. He hints at the self-preserving necessity of adopting a relativistic rather than an absolutist perspective in relation to moral and ethical dilemmas in his dangerous world, where law and order belong to the most powerful figures present at any given moment.

In McGee's case, which is instrumental in developing Easy's relativism more fully, Easy and Daphne arrive after the event, but there is plenty for him to describe and contemplate:

> There was a butcher's knife buried deep in his chest. The smooth brown haft stood out from his body like a cattail from a pond. He'd fallen with his back on a bunch of blankets so that the blood had flown upwards, around his face and neck. There was a lot of blood around his wide-eyed stare. Blue eyes and brown hair and dark blood so thick that you could have dished it up like Jell-O. My tongue grew a full beard and I gagged. (99-100)

As part of his emerging proximal investigator role, Easy resists the urge to vomit and instead collects a piece of evidence from the crime scene (a cigarette butt). As a mystery 'friend' of Daphne's at that moment in the narrative, and as a murder victim, the circumstances of whose death offer Easy potentially important evidence, this corpse of convenience is both a marker of motivation, in that we later discover that he's been blackmailing Daphne over her racial background, and also a motivator for Easy to save himself when he learns who the murderer is.

The road to self-preservation via McGee begins when Easy confronts Junior Fornay both with the information that the police have lifted a fingerprint from the knife, and with his own evidence of the Zapata brand cigarette butt: "'You the only one I know cheap enough to smoke this shit. And you see how somebody just let it drop to the floor and burn so that the paper on the bottom is just charred but not ash?'" (168), a habit Easy has observed Fornay engaging in at John's nightclub. Fornay explains that he drove McGee home when McGee offered him $100 to do so and to tell him how to find Daphne. But when they arrived, McGee asked him to give Frank Green a message before he would pay him the money: "He wanted me t'tell'im that him an' his friends had sumpin' on the girl'" (172). But all Fornay wanted was money, so McGee told him he could leave with $20 after he'd given him Daphne's friend, Coretta's name, and walk home from Laurel Canyon. When McGee went into another room, Fornay thought he was going to get a gun and so he armed himself with a kitchen knife, followed him in and stabbed him. Easy is shocked and asks Fornay, "'You just killed him 'cause he might'a hadda gun?'" (172). Easy's initial description and perception of Fornay as "a filthy man who didn't give a damn about anything" is proven to be accurate, but it gives Easy no satisfaction to confirm that he is correct: "He was sunken in his chair, like an old man. He disgusted me. He was brave enough to take on a smaller man, he was brave enough to stab an unarmed drunk, but Junior couldn't stand up to answer for his crimes. 'He ain't worf living,' the voice whispered in my head" (172).

The significance of the Voice's appearance and definitive judgment of Fornay becomes clear towards the end of the novel when Easy has to deal with the police detectives investigating McGee's death. They are convinced, since they can't identify the fingerprint on the knife, that Easy is the murderer and they will stop at nothing to have him convicted, even if they have to manufacture evidence. He suggests that they should determine if the fingerprint on the knife that killed McGee matches Junior Fornay's fingerprint, effectively issuing Fornay's death warrant. The measure of McGee's death has become, in Easy's hands as an observant proximal investigator and the potential victim of a racist police frame-up, a trade-off in which he must save himself by damning Junior Fornay. He has also witnessed Mouse's murder of Joppy Shag, but he takes no action that would result in Mouse's arrest for the crime, justifying his actions on both counts when he talks with his mentor of a kind, Odell Jones, a "quiet, religious man" (42), who has nothing to do with the criminal underworld Easy has been negotiating. Easy asks Odell,

> "If you know a man is wrong, I mean, if you know he did somethin' bad but you don't turn him in to the law because he's your friend, do you think that's right?"
>
> "All you got is your friends, Easy."
>
> "But then what if you knew somebody else who did something wrong but not so bad as the first man, but you turn this other guy in?"
>
> "I guess you figure that that other guy got ahold of some bad luck."
>
> We laughed for a long time. (219)

In *Devil in a Blue Dress*, there are multiple murders and therefore multiple corpses of convenience, and all of them, whether they are markers of motivation or motivators in themselves, or both, are compromised figures in that they have vested economic or strategic interests in finding Daphne Monet. It is difficult to summon much in the way of sympathy for any of them, other perhaps than Coretta Jones, who appears to fulfill the role of one of the 'innocent' victims of circumstance, a woman who couldn't have known how strong a motivator Daphne's stolen $30,000 would be for the "evil ones" she encountered, in particular in her case, Joppy Shag, who thought little of taking her life. Easy's relationship with Coretta as a friend ensures that Joppy's murder by Mouse will remain a mystery, unavenged, a corpse of convenience who won't live again or be remembered in any positive manner. In this novel, and in Cornwell's Post-Mortem, death may not be knowable, but it is watchable, observable, and measurable in different ways: physically, psychologically, economically, morally, and so on. It is also measurable in emotional terms, something that is represented largely negatively, that is, lovelessly, in the preceding examples, or which is made starkly obvious by the apparent absence of strong ties between the living and the dead. The harsh environment in which Rawlins exists is one where violent death is more or less expected, and life must go on where the strong, the street-smart, or the sharply observant and occasionally lucky ones, like Easy, are usually those who survive. In Cornwell's world of forensic deconstruction, the emphasis is on uncovering the psychopathology of the killer; horror, revulsion, and fear are the primary emotional responses elicited.

Other sub-genres and individual texts offer a broader range of emotional responses against which the knowability of death may be measured. I now focus on the corpse of convenience as an indicator or barometer of emotional involvement to argue for a continuum of emotional involvement along which we may locate particular victims as representative of the nature of sub-genres, or of individual texts, according to how the corpse of convenience is emotionally connected to particular members of the family of circumstance.

THE CORPSE OF CONVENIENCE AS A BAROMETER OF EMOTIONAL INVOLVEMENT

As we have observed, the investigator doesn't exist unless a crime occurs and, in contemporary crime fiction, corpses of convenience, performing a variety of tasks, litter the landscape, in keeping with Rule Seven of Van Dine's "Twenty Rules for Writing Detective Stories," published in 1928. Rule Seven states: "There simply must be a corpse in a detective novel, and the deader the corpse the better. No lesser crime than murder will suffice. Three hundred pages is far too much bother for a crime other than murder. After all, the reader's trouble and expenditure of energy must be rewarded" (190). This directive opens further lines of enquiry into the representation of the victims in contemporary murder texts. Its flippancy suggests murder as a game: "the deader the corpse the better." It gestures towards the effort of reading and the faith that the author must keep with the reader who is prepared to stay with a lengthy text: "the reader's trouble and expenditure of energy must be rewarded." But it also acknowledges the primary importance and relative superiority of this capital crime: "No lesser crime than murder will suffice." The narrator of Martin Amis's crime novel, Night Train, offers some reinforcement of this view and provides a comparative and emphatic summary:

Some say you can't top the adrenalin (and the dirty cash) of Narcotics, and all agree that Kidnapping is a million laughs (if murder in America is largely black on black, then kidnapping is largely gang on gang), and Sex Offenses has its followers, and Vice has its votaries, and Intelligence means what it says (Intelligence runs deep, and brings in the deepsea malefactors), but everyone is quietly aware that Homicide is the daddy. Homicide is the Show. (3)

We are offered murder as entertainment, murder as worthy of our reading efforts because it is the ultimate crime against the individual, and murder as the "daddy," the "Show," a graphic representation of death, usually as violent homicide.

Whatever the perspective – and all these are valid perspectives that fulfil the reader's horizon of murder fiction expectations – the site of proximity that is murder is very often simply a plot point which allows the investigator to proceed to other sites, such as race relations, corporate corruption, family or relationship dysfunction, or retribution and revenge. But even if some murders appear to be more expedient than others and are intended to be so, all murders in investigator-based, and other sub-genres of crime fiction involving murder, are plot points, the crème de la crème of plot points, the very reason for the narrative's existence, but plot points nonetheless. The victims are all, again, corpses of convenience, whatever the emotional investment of the reader in the character, or the emotional investment by other characters, particularly the proximal investigator, and whether or not the murder is of a village magistrate (Christie's The Murder at the Vicarage), or of an elderly couple at a Swedish farmhouse (Mankell's Faceless Killers), or of a young child on the roof of a Copenhagen warehouse (Miss Smilla's Feeling for Snow, by Høeg).

In this sense, the corpse of convenience can be approached from a range of positions along a continuum of emotional involvement from which one might derive a score or grief quotient. Such a score may provide one indicator of the nature of the sub-genre or text we are reading, and the characters with whom we're involved. The scale I have devised and from which this grief quotient emerges may be illustrated simply as follows:

Continuum of Emotional Involvement for Corpse of Convenience - Scale 1 - Grief
Grief Quotient (GQ) Scored by level of Emotional Involvement

Totally Expedient	Neither Expedient nor Catastrophic	Catastrophic Loss
|------------------	------------|------------	--------------------|
Low Grief (LGQ)	Neutral Response	High Grief (HGQ)

At the most expedient end of this scale, where a low grief quotient would be derived, we may locate the victim in Christie's clue-puzzle, The Murder at the Vicarage, Colonel Lucius Protheroe. He is depicted as a very unlikeable character living in St Mary Mead, and is a perfectly convenient corpse. Colonel Protheroe has a number of roles in the village including churchwarden and local magistrate and is, as the vicar says, "the kind of man who enjoys making a fuss on every conceivable occasion" (7). He is a person who easily alienates others because of his overbearing nature and controlling, arrogant personality. In only the second paragraph of the novel, the reader is invited to develop a complete lack of empathy with Protheroe when the vicar announces over lunch that "any one who murdered [him] would be doing the world at large a service" (5). Even Protheroe's daughter remarks, "if only father would be decent and die, I should be all right" (11), meaning she could collect her inheritance. Later, Protheroe's wife, Anne, confesses to the vicar that she is miserably and desperately unhappy in her marriage, is having an affair, and wishes the Colonel were dead (22). As is conventional in this sub-genre, several pieces of the clue puzzle related to the motivational set-up are brought into play prior to the murder. When the murder occurs, the grief quotient measurable in the responses of the other characters, is low and, by contrast, the level of attention directed towards solving the puzzle, a logical game of wits represented in the person of Marple, is very high. Reminding us of the nature of the story we are reading, the vicar observes, "In St. Mary Mead every one knows your most intimate affairs. There is no detective in England equal to a spinster lady of uncertain age with plenty of time on her hands"(25). What one wants to know is who did it, how, and why, and in the case of this particular story, when, because timing is crucial. Blinding grief or deep mourning are not generally obstacles to deduction in the clue-puzzle form, because they are virtually non-existent, except occasionally in the ritualistic form of funerals. Further, they are unnecessary to reader satisfaction, which is based in a detached reconstruction of the crime through the gathering and synthesising of clues, and the discarding of potential schools of red herrings.

Other types of murder novels, those that foreground depth of characterisation and relationships either equally with, or preferentially over complex plotting, enjoin the reader to engage with the victim in a deeply felt way, encouraging a strong degree of attachment, suggesting an inverse relationship between the grief quotient and the degree of expediency attributable to any given murder victim. In other words, the greater the expression of grief over the death, the lower the perception of the death as a mere plot point, and the closer we are brought to confronting our own mortality, albeit within the comfort zone of the controlled environment of the murder novel. Is it the case that the stronger this inverse relationship, the more likely the narrative is to succeed in fulfilling a reader's horizon of expectations of a given sub-genre, and therefore to be regarded as a worthy custom fit? In the clue-puzzle, as we have seen, the level of convenience or expediency is high and the grief quotient low. Contrast the position of Colonel Protheroe to that of Isaiah, the little boy in Miss Smilla's Feeling for Snow, who dies when he falls from the roof of a warehouse near his home as he flees a pursuer. Smilla describes the scene at his funeral, where the novel opens:

> Now they are lowering him into the ground. The coffin is made of dark wood, it looks so small, and there is already a layer of snow on it. The flakes are no bigger than tiny feathers, and that's the way snow is, it's not necessarily cold. What is happening at this moment is that the heavens are weeping for Isaiah, and the tears are turning into down of frost that is covering him up. In this way the universe is pulling an eiderdown over him, so that he will never again feel the cold. (4)

Immediately, one perceives a strong and loving relationship between Smilla and Isaiah, and this is reinforced throughout the novel as Smilla presents the story of how she met and came to be a kind of substitute mother to him. The casual intimacy of their relationship is apparent when she describes his response to receiving the gift of an anorak from her:

> I put the anorak on Isaiah, combed his hair, and then I lifted him up on to the lavatory seat. When he saw himself in the mirror, that's when it happened. The tropical fabric, the Greenlandic respect for fine clothes, the Danish joy in luxury all merged together. Maybe it also meant something that I had given it to him.
>
> A second later he had to sneeze.
>
> "Hold my nose!"
>
> I held his nose.
>
> "Why?" I asked. He usually blew his nose into the sink.
>
> As soon as I opened up my mouth, his eyes found my lips in the mirror.
>
> I often realized that he understood things even before they were expressed.
>
> "When I'm wearing annoraaq qaqortoq, this fine anorak, I don't want snot on my fingers." (68)

Smilla, remembering this moment as she stands at Isaiah's graveside with his mother, Juliane, is consumed by grief:

> For a brief instant my yearning comes on like madness. If only they would open the coffin for a moment and let me lie down beside his cold little body which someone has stuck a needle into, that they have opened up and photographed and cut slices out of and closed up again; if only once I could feel his erection against my thigh, a gesture of intimated, boundless eroticism, the beating of a moth's wing against my skin, the dark insects of happiness. (69)

It is Smilla's close relationship with the corpse of convenience, ahead of her desire to solve a game-like puzzle in the manner of a Miss Marple, which drives her to become a proximal investigator. She rejects the police view that his death was an accident because her feeling for snow tells her otherwise, and it is the depth of her despair that drives her to risk her life repeatedly. Isaiah, the strongest of emotional motivators for Smilla, is also revealed to be a marker of the motivations of many others, including the mechanic, Peter, who also loved him, but who has become involved in a complex conspiracy to profit from a meteorite found in Greenland and the Arctic worms it has caused to mutate into killer parasites. It is Isaiah's natural resistance to infection by these parasites, which killed his father some years before during an expedition to the meteorite's secret location, that has made him the centre of covert scientific attention and, therefore, a motivational marker for others. For Loyen, the pathologist and scientist, for example, Isaiah represents a scientific motivational marker, indicated most graphically by his taking a muscle biopsy from the boy post-mortem. The puncture mark through Isaiah's trousers and into his skin is among the first clues Smilla collects on her journey back to Greenland and the killer, who is also the main conspirator, Tørq. For Tørq, Isaiah is an inconvenience who possesses a potentially incriminating audio-cassette tape, his death an accident of circumstance caused by Isaiah's fear of him when chased up to the warehouse roof. But Isaiah is also an economic motivational marker pointing towards the meteorite, as Smilla discovers when she confronts Tørq and asks him why: "'Money .... Fame. More money .... It's the biggest scientific discovery of the century'" (404).

These examples illustrate that the corpse of convenience in a given narrative is capable of generating at least one, and sometimes more than one grief quotient on my Continuum of Emotional Involvement, and that these scores are influenced by how much we are able to learn about the victims, particularly through the eyes of others, and through the sets of relationships established within the family of circumstance. Isaiah's relationship with Smilla and, to a lesser extent, with Peter the mechanic, together with his status as an innocent and helpless child whose personality inspires affection and a desire to protect, are indicative of a high grief quotient. Colonel Protheroe's negative relationships with everyone and his unattractive persona are designed to lead us in the opposite direction. But as markers of the motivations of others, both Isaiah and Colonel Protheroe are flexible and suit the needs of the narrative, both structurally and as members of the family of circumstance. My intention here is not to extensively quantify the characters who are the victims in murder fiction, though others may wish to expand on my suggested scale, but rather to indicate the flexibility of the corpse of convenience in these texts, and to suggest that these characters remain the most important figures in these sub-genres because of their various motivational roles and their ability to generate love, distaste, and indifference in other characters and in readers.

But if I argue for a continuum of emotional involvement of this nature, and for particular types of custom fit success as one approaches each end of such a continuum, where might we locate the murder victims in the police procedural, or the private investigator text? Do they require a different interpretation of convenience, one that isn't so strongly related to deeply or superficially felt levels of grief, as to degrees of job satisfaction or performance? Proximal investigator Wallander, for instance, is a police officer because he can be nothing else. At one point in Faceless Killers, he contemplates having to find another job after he has been picked up for drink-driving by two of his colleagues, local police patrolmen. "He had explored the possibility that he might become head of security for some company. Or he might slip through the background check of some less choosy guard service. But his 20-year career with the police would be over. And he was a policeman to the core" (144). Wallander risks his life regularly in the performance of his duty, his health suffers, his marriage has failed, his daughter is estranged from him, and his father, though he never explains why, has hated his son's choice of career since the day he joined the force. But Wallander can't do anything else: his job is his life, and rather than a grief quotient arising along the continuum of emotional involvement, perhaps we may consider a performance score, in keeping with Wallander's colleague, Rydberg's assessment of the work they do. Even when they don't catch the criminals but know who they are, for Rydberg, "Justice doesn't only mean that the people who commit crimes are punished. It also means that we can never give up seeking the truth" (273). Here I suggest that instead of a grief quotient, we consider a satisfaction quotient on the Continuum of Emotional Involvement, which could be illustrated as follows:

Continuum of Emotional Involvement for Corpse of Convenience - Scale 2 - Satisfaction
Satisfaction/Performance Quotient (S/PQ) - Scored by level of Emotional Involvement

Totally Expedient	Neither Expedient nor Catastrophic	Catastrophic Loss
|---------------------	-----------|-----------	---------------------|
Low Satisfaction (LS/PQ)	Neutral Response	High Satisfaction (HS/PQ)

Throughout Faceless Killers, we are made aware of the intensity of Wallander's commitment to his vocation, even as he is anxious about and fearful of what he might discover about the first victims, an elderly couple attacked in their farmhouse and, later, a Somali refugee shot as he walks along a road, and their respective killers. His initial responses to the murders of the elderly couple are infused with fear as he reflects on how Swedish society is changing. When the police arrive at the farmhouse, they discover the old man is already dead, after being tortured: "His face was crushed beyond recognition. It looked as though someone had tried to cut off his nose. His hands were tied behind his back and his left thigh was shattered. The white bone shone against all that red" (10-11). The man's wife is still alive, but is tied to a chair and has a rope fashioned into a noose around her neck. When the neighbour walks into the bedroom, Wallander reacts angrily, telling the man to wait outside: "I'm yelling because I'm scared, he thought. What kind of world are we living in" (11)? The loss is catastrophic (and the potential job satisfaction very high if they capture the killers) because of the impact such a horrific crime will have on the local community and the country. And Wallander, fearing the unknown, follows the example of Poe's narrator in "The Man of the Crowd," describing the killers as "fiendish individuals" (15). Observations such as "He was feeling uneasy" (15), "He felt uneasy" (16), and "right now he felt uncertain and tired"(16), attest to Wallander's early misgivings but his professional training, his special personal assets of his mantra and occasional, accurate hunches, and his duty of care and responsibility as the lead investigator facilitate his ability to organise his team. "All of them were his colleagues. None of them was his close friend. And yet they were a team" (22). In this narrative of collective agency in an institutional setting, that is, the police force, the continuum of emotional involvement consists of the pursuit of murderers with the aim of achieving high levels of performance and performance satisfaction. This does not preclude, of course, levels of grief and personal involvement, but rather invites them as secondary sources of motivation. Wallander reacts at a visceral level of grief manifested through fear – he is uneasy and uncertain, and he knows he is yelling because he's afraid of what the crime might signify – to what he perceives as a society changing in negative ways. But as a police officer he is sworn to investigate and attempt to solve even the worst of crimes. The payoff is primarily job or performance satisfaction, along with the bonus of a slight, though equivocal, reduction in his anxiety and his sense of grieving for a Sweden that no longer exists, as the concluding lines of Faceless Killers illustrate: "he thought about the violence. The new era, which demanded a different kind of policeman. We're living in the age of the noose, he thought. Fear will be on the rise. He forced himself to push these thoughts aside and sought out the black woman of his dreams. The investigation was over. Now he could finally get some rest" (279).

Wallander's involvement with the corpses of convenience is dedicated and practically all-consuming, but this is only the case for the length of the particular investigation. His offering to the dead is the identification and capture of the murderers after which, in an offering to himself, he can "finally get some rest," having also acknowledged the troubling social changes that will continue to affect his profession, the unpredictability of the future represented by the unexplained noose placed around the neck of murder victim, Maria Lövgren. For proximal investigators like Jaspersen, however, unused to death in the form of murder, the boundaries are less clear-cut. At the end of Miss Smilla's Feeling for Snow, there is a fusion of Smilla's emotional involvement from the perspective of a highly charged personal investment in discovering the truth, with a realisation that, despite the crimes she has uncovered, including identifying the man responsible for Isaiah's death, there can be no definitive closure. In her description of chasing the murderer, Tørq, across the ice, Isaiah, or her memory of Isaiah, becomes an avenging siren who is one with the icy land- and seascapes:

> He's lost his bearings. He's being led out towards open water. Towards the spot where the current has hollowed out the ice so it's as thin as a foetal membrane, and under it the sea is dark and salty like blood, and a face is pressing up against the icy membrane from below; it's Isaiah's face, the as yet unborn Isaiah. He's calling Tørq. Is it Isaiah who is pulling him along, or am I the one who is trying to head him off and to force him towards the thin ice? (409)

It is possible to view Isaiah as Smilla's loved one and to confirm a very high level of grief following her catastrophic loss, but he also acts as a symbol of all Greenlanders, and of Greenland itself, a country colonised by Denmark, its people exploited and mistreated even to the point of murder, and its resources plundered. Isaiah wants blood, and he wants the chance to live again. Smilla manages to herd Tørq towards certain death, either in the ocean or as a frozen victim of the cold. But while her grief over Isaiah is deeply felt, she abrogates any satisfaction at having captured his killer by transferring credit to the weather, which, as she is fully aware with her special feeling for snow, will simply do its job: "He will only live a couple of hours. At some point he will stop, and the cold will transform him, like a stalactite, a frozen shell will close around a barely fluid life until even his pulse stops and he becomes one with the landscape. You can't win against the ice" (409). While Smilla makes definitive statements about her area of expertise, she is less certain in relation to the crimes that have been committed in pursuit of profit from the meteorite. Unlike Wallander, she is unable to effect a sense of closure for the authorities who will surely interrogate her, even temporarily, as she asserts in the brief coda which ends the novel: "Tell us, they'll come and say to me. So we may understand and close the case. They're wrong. It's only what you do not understand that you can come to a conclusion about. There will be no conclusion" (409). In more conventional murder novels, cases are closed, the dead acquire a kind of lifeblood as they are avenged successfully, the investigators, like Wallander, move to the next homicide, and the lie that Jackson asserts is at the heart of murder fiction, the illusion of the knowability of death through the corpse of convenience, is maintained and nourished.

The kind of maintenance and nourishment provided depends on quite a number of factors, as we have seen in the preceding examples, including the sub-genre represented, and the types of proximal investigators which populate the narratives, but also on the entire gathering of characters who form the cast of the novel, the family of circumstance, a family, as suggested in chapter one above, that is dependent on death in the form of the corpse of convenience for its life. I now turn to examples of the family of circumstance in investigator-based murder fiction, in particular in the works of Paretsky, and discuss how they contribute to the creation of custom fit texts, and a same-but-different genre reading experience.

"THE FAMILY IS THE CRADLE OF THE WORLD'S MISINFORMATION."

Don DeLillo, White Noise (81)

Googling the word, "family," on the Internet returns around three-quarters of a billion results. I mention this simply to demonstrate the pervasiveness of the word itself, and also to point to its popularity as a focus of discussion and interest, even though, somewhat surprisingly, I found relatively little of note dedicated to this subject in crime fiction theory and criticism. (Note 11: There is, however, an increasing number of texts and essays dedicated to analysing the highly successful television series *The Sopranos*, in particular in works by Gabbard, Greene and Vernezze, and Yacowar). During the twentieth century and for the first years of the twenty-first, the idea of the family has been challenged, defined and re-defined informally and formally, directly and indirectly including, for example, in the Australian Government's enactment of the Marriage Amendment Act in 2004. This Act – a response at Federal level to override State laws and prevent legal, State Government-sanctioned, same-sex marriages occurring in the Australian Commonwealth – defined a marriage as the union of a man and a woman exclusively, legally enforcing marriage as a heterosexual contract, a definition suggesting that the family unit originates only in heterosexual marriage. Previously, the Marriage Act hadn't specified the genders of marrying couples. But regardless of such legal sanctions, traditional definitions, and social pressure to conform, every kind of group that one can imagine has, at various times, been described as a family. Indeed, the word 'family,' in both literal and metaphorical senses, is more popular now than ever before to describe any group of two or more animate beings. Further, this essay so far is essentially a discussion of the family of characters that populate the murder text, and the boundaries within which they exist. Here, my interest lies in elaborating a little more specifically on this concept.

When I began reading for this essay I was struck by the presence in contemporary crime fiction of a wide range of what I understand as family groups. I have defined the word family for the purposes of this discussion as "any group of people connected by blood or other relationship," which allows for a broad but not meaningless range of groups to be taken into account. There must be a reason for members of these groups to be connected, a relationship or set of relationships within the group that can be delineated – even if these are not clear initially, which is usually the case, conveniently, in murder texts – in which the characters are gradually revealed to be connected through the corpse of convenience. In these texts I refer to the entire cast of characters present as the family of circumstance, which also equates to the cast of suspects including, of course, the proximal investigator. (Note 12: Early in my research for this essay, I initially planned to use the terms 'family of convenience' and 'corpse of circumstance,' but decided that 'family of circumstance' and 'corpse of convenience' more accurately reflected the direction I wanted to take with my argument. Later on, out of curiosity, I searched the Internet for other instances of the term's use and discovered a moderate number of examples – only about four on Google, but up to 30 or so on Yahoo (some of these are variations on the same themes). One example that encapsulates the term's broader applicability appears on the website of the Associated Retired Aviation Professionals in relation to the crash of TWA flight 800 in July, 1996, off Long Island, New York, in which all on board perished. The article's author, Patrick Healy, refers to a small group of victims' family members, friends, and associates, who gather each year to remember their loved ones. Healy quotes the father of a victim, who describes the group as a "family of circumstance" because, he explains: "'Two hundred and thirty people were on an aircraft together. That's why we're friends. It's what put us together'"). Since the proximal investigator is the main character in investigator-based murder fiction, whether of the series or one-off variety, I view these suspects, as individuals and groups, from the investigator's perspective. They incorporate members of the family of origin and family of choice of the proximal investigator, and members of what may be most conveniently described as the family of the text: the extra characters associated with the investigation, since we assume that life for the proximal investigator with their usual families of origin and choice goes on beyond the text we read, and was already established before this particular narrative arose. In the case of series-based novels, we anticipate that more of this life will be offered in textual form in subsequent instalments. The family of circumstance includes, importantly, the corpse of convenience, and I elaborate on this inclusion below. These family groups have porous borders. Frequently some of their members can be seen to perform multiple roles, identifiable as members of several family groups within the family of circumstance. For instance, as I discuss shortly, Boom Boom Warshawski, proximal investigator V. I.'s cousin, is a member of the family of the text, a member of V. I.'s family of origin who has also become a member of her family of choice (they continue an adult friendship with each other independent of, but originating in their childhood blood ties as cousins), and Boom Boom is the first and primary corpse of convenience in Deadlock.

Some of these characters, as mentioned, will be eliminated as suspects almost instantly as those possessing means, motive, and opportunity are gradually foregrounded, but my perspective follows criminal investigative procedure: everyone begins life in the investigation as a suspect, including the proximal investigator and the corpse of convenience, and there are examples that confirm that this approach is warranted. Regarding the victim, for example, the corpse of convenience in Trent's Last Case by E. C. Bentley, Sigsbee Manderson, plots his own attempted murder in order to set up and condemn his business associate, who is also his wife's lover, Jack Marlowe. But a complication involving a third party results in Manderson's death rather than his wounding, and a cover-up ensues, leaving the corpse of convenience effectively complicit in his own demise. In Crais' Elvis Cole mystery, The Forgotten Man, detective Kelly Diaz, the off-duty police officer who finds the body of George Reinnike (alias Payne Keller) in an alley near Skid Row and remains, as a member of the police team, a proximal investigator in the case, is also, in fact, Reinnike's murderer. She takes revenge for Reinnike's murder of her parents and brother when she was four years old. Another, more famous instance of a proximal investigator as a murderer, occurs in Christie's Curtain: Poirot's Last Case. The subtitle of this novel points to at least one outcome: the Belgian is found dead in bed from natural causes (160) shortly after he has dispatched the sadistic villain, Stephen Norton. Poirot confesses to the shooting in a last letter to his close friend, confidant and Watson-like figure, Captain Arthur Hastings, who has failed to recognise, among other clues, the telltale sign of the perfectly symmetrical shot to Norton's forehead as indicative of Poirot's obsessive need for order: "I should, I am aware, have shot him through the temple. I could not bring myself to produce an effect so lop-sided, so haphazard .... Oh Hastings, Hastings, that should have told you the truth" (186).

Examples such as these act as precedents that justify the inclusion of both the proximal investigator and the corpse of convenience in the family of circumstance. Indeed, it is these two character roles that dictate the makeup of this family and its sub-groups, so how does the family of circumstance operate in the murder narrative to achieve a custom fit? To begin with biology, in contemporary investigator-based murder fiction, as we have already seen, relationship dysfunction at the level of the family of origin of the proximal investigator is frequently the rule rather than the exception, and it is this shaky foundation that leads many proximal investigators to leave, or reduce contact with their families of origin and instead establish families of choice. Of course, the proximal investigator may also return to, revel, or languish in such dysfunction as a means of developing further dramatic or comedic tension (Janet Evanovich's Stephanie Plum series is a good example of the latter, with Plum's proximal investigations arising from her role as a bounty hunter whose families of origin and choice inevitably help and hinder her investigations). The members of both these groups, origin and choice, often perform valuable services during the course of investigations. In fact, they are tailor-made for the purpose of aiding and abetting, or even saving the life of the proximal investigator, applying their various skills, connections, and allegiances to the goal of solving murders. In addition, they are also significant figures in that their relationships with the proximal investigator contribute to further elucidation of this character's personality, perspectives, and lifestyle. In so doing, they reinforce one of the hallmarks of much contemporary investigator-based murder fiction, which places equal or near equal emphasis on the investigator's life along with the investigations they undertake, a kind of symmetry less obsessively sought than Poirot's version perhaps, but equally as compelling. Such narrative digressions from the path of pure investigation contribute to differentiating proximal investigators as unique and fresh, especially in the confines of generic convention.

The writers of series-based novels, such as Paretsky, develop evolving proximal investigators with the aim of their achieving the status of three-dimensional, fully rounded characters. Although Warshawski is a hard-boiled private eye in the tradition of Spade and Marlowe, when she walks the frequently mean and nasty streets of Chicago, backup isn't far away in the form of members of her families of origin and choice. The most important members of her family of origin, her parents, Tony and Gabriella, are deceased, but her dreams and memories of them continue to exert considerable influence over her life throughout the series and offer insights into her approach to family obligations and how she conducts herself and her investigations. Gill Plain suggests that, although the orphaned V. I. appears to be a solitary figure suggestive of "interwar models of the detective as existing in a familial vacuum" (145), the "spectral presence" of V. I.'s parents helps to create a "curious transitional model that manages both to have its family and eat it," too (145).

Accompanying the parental spectres in a number of the novels is a sprinkling of living relatives, members of V. I.'s extended family of origin but effectively members of the family of the text, who are responsible for drawing her into murderous circumstances that push her towards taking up investigations: Aunt Elena Warshawski in Burn Marks, for instance, or Aunt Rosa Vignelli in Killing Orders. In the latter novel, it is a promise V. I., at the age of 15, made to her dying mother that connects her to Aunt Rosa and the investigation that follows when Rosa contacts her and asks for help: "she made me promise to help Rosa if her aunt ever needed me. I had tried to argue with Gabriella: Rosa hated her, hated me – we had no obligation. But my mother insisted and I could not refuse" (15). In this novel, the proximal investigator's family of origin, including deceased members, plays a vital role in kick-starting the murder story and telling us about V. I.'s ethics and her standing as an honourable individual. This is the also the case with several other novels in the series, including the second, Deadlock, which begins with the funeral and wake for her cousin, Boom Boom who, it transpires, has died in circumstances initially written-off as an accidental death. Here, again, there is a blending of investigative practice with information about the investigator's family background and relationships, which give further insights into the character of V. I. as a person, and proximal investigator, of substance. Boom Boom's funeral and wake are opportunities for V. I. to provide the reader with information about herself and her relatives, and where she stands in the scheme of family of origin matters. She is Boom Boom's executor, but since she was out of town when he died, his extensive network of aunts (his mother is dead) made the burial arrangements, allowing V. I. to tell us, as she sits in St Wenceslas Church with Boom Boom's "moist, indistinguishable aunts and cousins,"(10) that "[n]either of my parents had been religious. My Italian mother was half Jewish, my father Polish, from a long line of skeptics. They'd decided not to inflict any faith on me, although my mother always baked me little orecchi dÁman at Purim"(10).

The proceedings are held in the old neighbourhood, which is filled with relatives of one variety or another, offering the opportunity to position V. I. as largely estranged from this sprawling group, to identify Boom Boom as one true friend who emerges from the pack of "moist" kin, and to introduce an important and in many respects, exemplary member of her parents' family of choice, and by extension,

V. I.'s. Bobby Mallory is a police officer who worked with her father and was his friend. He acts towards V. I. as a kind of substitute father, on occasion, and he is the only person she allows to call her 'Vicki,' as her parents did. But Mallory is truly of her parents' generation and, although V. I. conveniently calls upon him from time to time for help because of his active policing role and influence with police authorities, he can also be a frustrating, interfering presence who believes that the job of a private eye is totally inappropriate for a woman. In Killing Orders, V. I. sums up this attitude when Mallory is obligated to return her gun after an incident in another police jurisdiction: "It hurt Bobby physically to tell me about the gun. He didn't want me carrying it, he didn't want me in the detective business, he wanted me in Bridgeport or Melrose Park with six children and, presumably, a husband"(178).

Mallory's attitudes are a useful means by which Paretsky can create a variety of scenes and narrative sub-plots throughout the series that reveal more about V. I.'s character and tackle contentious social issues. In some of these novels, though, he appears as more of a straw man representative of outdated and bigoted ideas, although this occasional authorial heavy-handedness also encourages speculation about how Mallory established and maintained such a strong friendship with V. I.'s father, Tony, who V. I. venerates as a noble and almost saintly figure, presumably incapable of malice or unfairness. It is no coincidence, of course, that the series-based novel is well-positioned to exploit such a relationship repeatedly and to change its dynamics from one novel in the series to the next. Perhaps Mallory unsuccessfully aspired to be like his friend, and also sees the same qualities in his friend's daughter, but what did Tony see in Mallory and why, except out of familial loyalty, does V. I. continue to engage with this frequently obnoxious man? On the other hand, for how long will Mallory wear a hairshirt in memory of Tony and subject himself to grudgingly protecting Tony's wayward – from Mallory's perspective – daughter?

The possible explanation is guilt combined with a sense of providing a replacement parental figure, however inadequate he may be to the task. "'You know, Tony Warshawski was one of my best friends,'" he tells V. I. after she has survived another attempt on her life in Killing Orders. "'Anything happens to you, his and Gabriella's ghosts will haunt me the rest of my life'" (135). Mallory's attitudes in Killing Orders, however, incorporate a generalised anti-feminist misogyny and ingrained, malicious homophobia. When, provoked by the victim's mother, he interrogates V. I. about the murder of her old friend, Agnes Paciorek, the daughter of influential and wealthy Chicago Catholics, he provides the reader with historical information about V. I., confirms her political positions on war and abortion, invokes V. I.'s father's name to encourage guilt in V. I., presumes she has had an affair with Agnes, and clearly demonstrates his bias:

> Mallory clenched his fist tightly around the edge of his metal desk. "You and Paciorek were lesbians, weren't you?" Suddenly his control broke and he smashed his fist on the desk top. "When Tony was dying you were up at the University of Chicago screwing around like a pervert, weren't you? It wasn't enough that you demonstrated against the war and got involved with that filthy abortion underground. Don't think we couldn't have pulled you in on that. We could have, a hundred times over. But everyone wanted to protect Tony. You were the most important thing in the world to him, and all the time – Jesus Christ, Victoria. When I talked to Mrs. Paciorek this morning, I wanted to puke. (76)

This outburst gives V. I. the opportunity to respond in a way that clearly establishes her perspective for the reader: "'First of all, under the Illinois criminal code, lesbianism between consenting adults is not an indictable offense. Therefore it is none of your goddamned business whether or not Ms. Paciorek and I were lovers. Second, my relations with her are totally unconnected with your murder investigation"(77). But beyond this, Mallory's interrogation provokes V. I. to ask him why he would "'believe a shopping list of calumny'" from Agnes's mother, "'without even asking me, and you've known me since I was born'" (77), and it inspires V. I. to eventually elaborate to Mallory on her friendship with Agnes which arose and developed at a particular time in V. I.'s life, so that the reader then learns more about V. I.'s activities during her student days, further enhancing the development of, and differentiating the character as more than simply a gumshoe for the crime du jour.

In this novel, in contrast to V. I.'s position – as a more or less fearless, independent operator – and the action she takes which endangers her life, Mallory, the product of collectivist thinking and manipulation, demonstrates a fear of challenging established institutional authority, whether police (in the form of the FBI) or religious (the Catholic Church and, by association, the wealthy Paciorek family), and an almost slavish devotion to stereotypical law enforcement. This depiction reinforces the proximal investigator's primacy as the series standard-bearer in terms of ethics, bravery, loyalty, and countless other positive attributes. Further, Mallory's in loco parentis attitudes handily contrast with the less controlling and far less condemnatory perceptions of V. I.'s downstairs neighbour, retired machinist, Sal Contreras – "the dog, his cooking, and I make up the bulk of his entertainment" (Toxic 33) – whose overriding concern is for V. I.'s safety. He is someone V. I. allows into her life independently of family of origin connections, with their friendship originating in their living in the same apartment building, a move which is briefly sketched near the end of Killing Orders (230) and heralds his appearance in the next novel, Bitter Medicine. Like other members of her ongoing, small family of choice, Contreras – along with V. I.'s best friend, Dr Lottie Herschel, and journalist Murray Ryerson – performs a variety of roles: a parental figure of sorts, supportive neighbour and friend, dog-sitter, cook and source of cases (V. I. investigates the death of his old workmate and friend, Mitch Kruger in Guardian Angel). Occasionally, he is a life-saver when she drops off his sometimes intrusive radar and he mounts a search and rescue mission for her with their shared dog, Peppy (Toxic 176).

There is even an opportunity for Peppy, usually a dependent member of V. I.'s family of choice, to act as a maternal figure when V. I. is rescued: "The dog looked at me anxiously, then started to lick my face – I was her long-lost puppy found in the nick of time. All the while that Mr Contreras freed my hands, rubbing some semblance of circulation back into my arms, she kept washing my face" (176).

V. I.'s human mother substitute is Lottie Herschel who, as a young Viennese Jewish woman, fled from Nazi Europe and became a doctor. She runs a highly successful medical practice as well as a free clinic for the poor, knows many influential figures in Chicago society circles, and is a long-time friend and medical practitioner, as well as a surrogate mother to V. I.: "'You are the daughter of my heart, Victoria. I know it's not the same as having Gabriella, but the love is there'" (Toxic 221). And again, in Killing Orders: "'You have been the daughter I never had, V. I. As well as one of the best friends a woman could ever desire'" (231-32). Lottie can be as frustrating and difficult in her own way as Mallory is, coming from his milieu into V. I.'s life. In keeping with the theme of loyalty and betrayal in Killing Orders, Lottie, like Mallory, doubts V. I.'s integrity for a while when she suspects that V. I. knows more about her Uncle Stefan than she has admitted (54-54), even though they have known each other as close friends for decades. And Lottie, like members of V. I.'s family of origin, is also a source of investigations (Total Recall). While Mallory does his best to deter V. I. from her investigative pursuits, Lottie can be counted upon to provide friends or relatives to assist V. I.'s research. In Killing Orders, for instance, Lottie's Uncle Stefan, an engraver and convicted forger, takes a pivotal role in V. I.'s investigation into forged stock certificates which hint at a much larger conspiracy and threaten to destroy her Aunt Rosa's life.

In this novel, members of a number of disparate family-style groups interact in a complex story of corruption at the highest levels of the Roman Catholic Church and Chicago society. Paretsky takes real-life scandals, of the Vatican's Banco Ambrosiano and Roberto Calvi's theft of a billion dollars from the bank, to develop a narrative that, in part, implicates the Catholic Church, the Mafia, the FBI, and other law enforcement agents in a coverup.

In this story, as in many others in the series, V. I. relies on the journalist, Murray Ryerson, who has also been her occasional lover. Murray accompanies her on some of her investigations so that he acquires eyewitness knowledge; he undertakes research; and he publishes stories at strategic points to protect her or other characters by revealing criminal activities, provoking further movement in the narrative or contributing to the plot's resolution. Her old friend, Freeman Carter, a lawyer in her ex-husband's law firm, and another recurring character in her family of choice, bails her out of jail and smoothes the way for her to maintain a clean record and avoid Mallory's attempts to have her private investigator's licence revoked (231). Roger Ferrant, who appeared in Deadlock, reappears in Killing Orders as both lover and insurance executive; he provides V. I. with access to information she would otherwise be unable to obtain, as well as engaging in a brief affair with her and offering her temporary accommodation in his hotel suite when her apartment is firebombed. He is also the corporate figure who ensures that she is paid a large fee for her investigations on behalf of his insurance company, a fee which, when combined with the $25,000 in cash she receives anonymously (she knows it is effectively hush money from Mafia Don Pasquale in gratitiude for information she supplied to him, but the ethical V. I. is able to accept it when it arrives without formal identification of its origin), facilitates her move to the apartment complex where she meets Sal Contreras.

The relationships Paretsky establishes for V. I. to participate in as orphan, relative, friend, sometime lover, partner, pet owner, or professional investigator, begin with her families of origin and choice, and grow to embrace the family of the text, whose most significant members, the corpses of convenience, in part dictate the ways, unique to any given text, in which these relationships play out. In Killing Orders, the family of circumstance is a perfect cradle of misinformation which eventually results in clarity in V. I.'s investigative hands. The narrative places an emphasis on issues of loyalty and betrayal, of the loss of faith, belief, and trust by and among family members, at the level of individual relationships and in their interaction with religious and corporate institutions. But it also emphasises the restoration of these values, for some members, in forms modified by new knowledge brought about by trauma and painful revelations. Warshawski, the proximal investigator, may be viewed as an independent agent in her role as a private eye, but she also operates in a collective manner, similar to police agents through her informal networks of relatives, friends, information bringers, experts, and miscellaneous temporary acquaintances.

In their quest for the custom fit, other series-based proximal investigators present equally complex networks of relationships as those I have discussed in relation to Warshawski. The family of circumstance in Mankell's Faceless Killers presents a proximal investigator's family of origin whose members are more likely to impede Wallander's investigative progress than contribute positively to it, reinforcing the strength of his commitment to his vocation as a policeman and his relationship with most members of his family of choice who consist of the investigative team and support staff at his police station. But at the same time, his interactions with his father, daughter, estranged wife, sister, and a few other family of choice friends not associated with the police, are also integral to the plot. Like Warshawski's families of origin and choice, they provide background to Wallander's life, shades of colour to his personality and, despite the apparently rampant negativity, a relatively relieving contrast to the dark nature of the murder investigations with which he is involved. In this first novel of the series, Wallander's marriage is over, his daughter has no interest in maintaining a relationship of any value with him, his wife demands a divorce, he realises that he has grown away from both his sister and his oldest friend and, as a bonus, his father is beginning to show signs of dementia. He does, however, have his work, and it is to this work, frightening and demanding as it is, that he turns in order to restore momentum and purpose to his life. His level of professional and emotional involvement with the corpses of convenience reflects his commitment to the collective, and to himself as an individual whose vocation is policing. At the end of Faceless Killers, the anticipation is that his families of origin and choice will move with him into his next investigtion.

There is also a strong vocational aspect in the journey proximal investigator Jaspersen undertakes in Miss Smilla's Feeling for Snow, even though Smilla has no formal connection with private investigative or police work. She is an amateur with extraordinary skills and personality traits perfectly suited to searching for the killer of her young friend and family of choice member, Isaiah, the corpse of convenience who determines the course of her life for some time, inspiring a vocation-like passion to solve the mystery and the crime.

Like Warshawski, Smilla's dead mother, a Greenlander, is a strong presence in her life but her father, Moritz, who is alive, is primarily a source of monetary sustenance and, because of his fame, facilitates some of her movements through Danish society. Smilla's family of choice is limited to Isaiah, his mother Juliane, and Peter, the mechanic, who looks after the maintenance of their apartment building, and with whom Smilla has an affair. The broader family of circumstance consists of characters who develop the narrative as they simultaneously contribute to our understanding of Smilla the person, although there is no suspicion that this is anything other than a one-off text, despite Smilla's final observation that "there will be no conclusion."

Exactly the opposite impression is created at the end of the Rawlins novel, Devil in a Blue Dress, which establishes a future for Easy with money, his house secured, and the little boy he saved from the paedophiles safe and awaiting Easy's return, with Easy's Mexican friend, Primo. Primo is a temporary member of Easy's family of choice in an era, according to Easy, "before ancestry had been discovered [when] a Mexican and a Negro considered themselves the same. That is to say, just another couple of unlucky stiffs left holding the short end of the stick" (181). Easy moves from sacked worker to amateur investigator hired by DeWitt Albright, to a self-described detective as he searches for Daphne Monet and the gangster, Frank Green (134). But as aeroplane mechanic, amateur or semi-professional detective, Easy's family of origin is absent, an absence that goes unremarked, and his family of choice presents some stark choices. His best friend, who has saved his life in the past (33) is a psychopath, Raymond 'Mouse' Alexander, someone who "could put a knife in a man's stomach and ten minutes later sit down to a plate of spaghetti" (55). Easy had an affair with Mouse's now-estranged wife, Etta Mae, when she and Mouse were engaged. Mouse found out about it "but he didn't care. Mouse never worried about what his women did. But if I'd touched his money he'd have killed me straight away" (157). And Mouse is the reason Easy left Houston for Los Angeles after he killed his (Mouse's) stepbrother, a crime for which Easy believes Mouse should have died. Mouse also kills a so-called friend of Easy's, Joppy Shag, who murdered Coretta James, a friend of Daphne Monet. Easy rationalises Mouse's behaviour by deciding that "Joppy had been my friend but I'd seen many men die and I cared for Coretta too" (206). Easy falls into a brief but passionate sexual relationship with Daphne Monet, a member of the family of the text who becomes a temporary member of his family of choice, and a woman he describes as "death herself" (208). But even so, at the end of the novel, despite his relief that she is leaving town with her share of the money, his desire for her is such that he "would have taken her in a second if she'd asked me to" (208). The only apparently stable member of Easy's family of choice is Odell Jones, an older man who is a father figure and mentor of sorts, a sounding board as discussed previously in this chapter, against whom Easy tests the integrity or otherwise of his actions and decisions. In a sense, though, perhaps it is Easy's Voice, which appears when Easy and Daphne discover the murdered Richard McGee, that is his best friend, his higher self, protecting him in extreme situations, trustworthy, and with only Easy's best interests at heart.

The range of crime fiction and, specifically, investigator-based murder texts available to readers today reflects, illustrates, and emphasises their connections with society in many different ways; the depiction of family groups is one of these ways. Seemingly disparate characters are brought together to form proximal investigators' families of choice, which may include members of their families of origin, and members of the family of the text. They perform under the umbrella of the family of circumstance and contribute to the challenge of expanding readers' horizons of expectation which, in turn, contribute to the evolution of the genre. Readers respond to texts on many levels, including the desire for basic entertainment and vicarious thrills, the hope of seeing people like themselves represented as characters, the need to confirm and reinforce their social, moral, religious, or political views, or to challenge status quos in these areas and proffer alternative worlds. Authors such as Paretsky, Mankell, Høeg, Mosley, and many others present complex characters whose stories may be enjoyed at the level of entertainment, but they also address a range of concerns relating to issues such as gender discrimination, racism, immigration, refugees, poverty, colonialism, and corrupt corporate, government and social power elites, among others. The perspectives from which they present these issues by engaging with the members of their families of circumstance is a further means of achieving the custom fit text.

As a reader, writer, and researcher engaging with investigator-based murder fiction fairly constantly over several years and, before this, as a reader of general crime fiction, I have identified a strong personal link with some of the political aspects of these texts, a link which is unsurprising when I offer the information that I have been associated with politics, politicians, and their parties, since childhood, at first through my father's union activities and involvement as a party member and a political candidate with the Australian Labor Party, the Queensland Labor Party, and the Democratic Labor Party, and then through my own interest. At the beginning of this section on the family of circumstance, I alluded to the Australian Government's enactment of the Marriage Amendment Act 2004, which affords access to legal marriage only for heterosexual couples. I referred to this Act's specificity to illustrate the fact that, despite such restrictive legislative imprimaturs, families will form, no matter what disadvantaging impediments may arise, legal or otherwise, in relation to unions such as marriage, a traditionally-accepted fore-runner to the creation of family units. Some of the manoeuvring behind this legislation – manoeuvring which also significantly affected the 2004 Federal election, held on October 9, and its outcomes – undertaken by Australia's extended political family, comprising the groups that form our recognised major and minor political parties, is worth noting as a means of general comparison with the family of circumstance as it forms and develops in investigator-based murder fiction. This strand of contentious political narrative embedded in the 2004 election, based as it was in the 'family values' debate, also had a direct impact on my decision to use the word 'family' of circumstance, rather than group, cast, crowd, team, or any other collective descriptor.

At this election, the Family First Party stood candidates for the first time. The Party's web site at the time offered no definition of 'family', but when asked on ABC Radio National's Religion Report how the Party defined 'family' and 'family values,' founder Andrew Evans said, "Mums and Dads, Grandpas and Grandmas, boys and girls, heterosexual, singles" ("Family First Founder"). Although Mr Evans did not specifically address the definition of 'family values,' the Party's web site at the time indicated that it would oppose "any legislation that will be hurtful to families" ("Who We Are" np) and, during the Religion Report interview, Mr Evans reiterated this when asked what he was against: "anything that hurts the families" ("Family First Founder"), he said.

Further clarification of the Family First Party's perception of what a family consists of – and in – was provided by the party's Queensland Senate candidate, John Lewis. Four days before the election, Lewis indicated that, despite a previously agreed preference deal with the Federal Coalition, the Liberal candidate for the seat of Brisbane, Ingrid Tall, would not receive his party's preferences because of her sexual orientation. Lewis said that Tall "did not fit the profile of a basic unit of family – which involved a man and a woman" ("Family First Refuses" np). Tall then lived with her female partner, and also cared for her father in the same household.

Sitting North Queensland Liberal MP Warren Entsch, who supports gay marriage and who voted with the Australian Greens (Greens) and Australian Democrats (Democrats) against the Marriage Amendment Act 2004, was also denied the Family First party's preferences. The Marriage Amendment Act 2004 specifically defines marriage as "the union of a man and a woman to the exclusion of all others, voluntarily entered into for life" (Marriage 3). However, Family First indicated that it would swap preferences with the Liberal MP for Parramatta, Ross Cameron who, in September 2004, publicly announced that he had engaged in an extra-marital affair while his wife was pregnant with twins ("Family First Refuses" np).

On the 23rd of September, 2004, the Sydney Star Observer reported that openly gay Democrat Senator Brian Grieg (for Western Australia) would swap preferences with the Family First party in a bid to achieve re-election. The then Democrats leader, Senator Andrew Bartlett, indicated that Family First and the Democrats agreed on some issues and that the Democrats and Greens disagreed on a number of policies (Farrar np). Brian Greig was defeated. Family First managed, because of a preference deal with the Australian Labor Party (ALP) in Victoria which excluded the Greens candidate, to have a Senator elected. Even though the Greens outpolled Family First by five-to-one and even though Family First achieved only 1.9% of the primary vote, the preference deal ensured that the Family First candidate, Steve Fielding, would receive 220,216 preferences from the ALP's Senator Jacinta Collins in the 285th and final round of counting ("Family First Senator" np). Notwithstanding the obvious and cliched conclusion that politics makes strange bedfellows, this series of interactions and exchanges suggests that it is in the nature of political parties and their members to exhibit bias towards their own public and private party platforms while simultaneously appearing frequently to contradict the reasons for their very creation and continued existence.

They are rather like families in this respect and, certainly, they arguably resemble in many ways the family of circumstance as I conceive of it in investigator-based murder texts and as I developed it in "Thicker Than Water." My personal experience of political parties and their frequently dysfunctional dynamics, both within and across organisations, probably influenced my depictions of primary characters and their interrelationships in "Thicker Than Water," but exactly to what extent this may be the case, I would hesitate to speculate. To be around or involved in a phenomenon like party politics from a very early age can result in a politically-filtered perspective developing as a kind of second – and therefore, frequently unnoticed – nature. A further question that suggests itself here is how different is the world of political families of circumstance from how most relatively dysfunctional families – and there are those who would argue that most families are relatively dysfunctional – behave? Perhaps not very different at all. In the context of "Thicker Than Water" and its family of circumstance, as with other investigator-based murder texts, there are motivations and counter-motivations, false leads and dead ends; love, trust, friendship, loss, and betrayal; contradictions, deceptions, and manipulations. All these and more challenges – physical, psychological, and ethical – are placed in the proximal investigator's path as she manoeuvres to complete the quest, solve the crime, and identify the most traitorous member of the family of circumstance, thus creating a new level of equilibrium and delivering to the corpse of convenience, and the reader, the longed-for blood of justice, and the redemptive power of truth revealed.

Conclusion

This essay has been an exploration of how character roles in the form of the proximal investigator, the corpse of convenience, and the family of circumstance contribute to the creation of custom fit murder texts, texts which offer a same-but-different crime reading experience. These terms emerged from my reading of, and research into crime fiction, in particular investigator-based murder fiction, and the central question of the essay arose as I researched and wrote my novel, "Thicker Than Water." The proximal investigator, as discussed in chapter two, describes a multitude of investigative types: private eye, police detective, amateur sleuth, forensic and other scientific, sociological, and psychological investigators, as well as the broadest diversity of characters in relation to such demographic factors as gender, ethnicity, religion, occupation, age, socio-economic, and sexual orientation. I have argued that what these investigators all have in common is their proximity to the crime or crimes of the text which, in the case of murder texts, is their proximity to the corpse or corpses of convenience, the murder victims whose depiction, no matter how perfunctory or how deeply felt, is ultimately and always a plot point without which the narrative cannot exist. The proximal investigator and the corpse of convenience are the pivotal characters whose presence facilitates the emergence of all the other characters in the text, the group for whom I have coined another generic term: the family of circumstance. I considered the family of circumstance from the point of view of the proximal investigator who is, as I have argued, and regardless of the plot point significance of the corpse of convenience, the most important character in the text. This family consists of the members of the investigator's families of origin and choice, and the remaining members of the cast of characters, in effect, the members of the family of the text. As illustrated, individual characters can fulfil roles in each of these families, and it is in the representation of all these characters and their network of relationships that the custom fit text is formed as the narrative proceeds.

In this essay, I have demonstrated the efficacy of my three terms: proximal investigator, corpse of convenience, and family of circumstance, particularly by reading the works of Paretsky, Høeg, Mosley, and Mankell. Others may adopt these terms in their own analysis of investigator-based murder texts in order to further demonstrate their worth, or otherwise, as generic terms that can bring together a very wide range of characters across a number of crime fiction subgenres to determine their commonalities and their differentiating features. Employing both diachronic and synchronic approaches may highlight the evolutionary nature of the genre, and its demand for constant innovation and experimentation. When Paretsky published her first Warshawski novel, Indemnity Only, in 1982, she was part of a vanguard of feminist authors, including Muller, Liza Cody, Grafton, and Barbara Wilson, writing characters who challenged representations of the hard-boiled detective successfully established half a century earlier by Hammett and Marlowe as a response to what they perceived as unrealistic British cosies featuring "detectives of exquisite and impossible gentility."

Paretsky embraces many of the conventions of the hard-boiled genre, but adds her own unique twists in pursuit of the custom fit: a female, idealistic rather than cynical private eye with expertise in financial fraud and corporate malfeasance. Her dreams, and sometimes nightmares, are not of villains captured or heroic deeds performed but of her mother, Gabriella, whose precious wine goblets she risks her life to save, and whose diamond drop earrings she wears to fancy Chicago society events. She has a small but reliable and stable family of choice, whose members are uniquely and conveniently placed, through their particular skills, experience, and connections, to assist her investigations. This supportive core group is occasionally augmented by temporary additions in one or more individual instalments, and what this family of choice, along with the larger family of circumstance created by each individual text does is to further enhance the standing of the proximal investigator as a unique character with whom we wish to travel on her quests. Once she becomes involved with the corpse of convenience – whether or not that involvement is at the high or low end of emotional investment or performance satisfaction – in accordance with the conventions of the genre, there can be no withdrawal or refusal of the call to investigate. In each novel we learn some new information to supplement our existing knowledge; each outing with V. I. is the same in its approach to time-honoured investigative, gumshoeing conventions, but slightly different in its revelations about both V. I. and the other major ongoing characters. This is a pattern followed by other authors when establishing proximal investigators in their geographic, socio-economic, political, and cultural milieus, from Crais' Elvis Cole series set in Los Angeles, with Cole and his business partner Joe Pike supplemented by Cole's complicated private life, to Mankell's series with Wallander which, in an interesting development, features Wallender's daughter, Linda – who also appears in earlier instalments – joining him in Ystaad as a police officer in Before the Frost. Grafton's Kinsey Milhone novels, over time, have differentiated themselves not only because of the character of Kinsey with her unique collection of traits and her family groups (including dead parents), but because Grafton's novels have remained in the 1980s in fictional Santa Teresa (the location itself is a homage to Ross McDonald's Santa Teresa) without the benefit, among other advances, of mobile phones, the Internet, highly-refined forensic science, or computerised databases of criminal records.

Introducing her collection of essays, Slouching towards Bethlehem, Joan Didion asserts that "writers are always selling somebody out"(14). Her emphasis ensures that we, the readers, understand its importance. In the context of crime fiction, the writers who have helped the genre evolve in one way or another, have not sold out any body, but rather have positively embraced writing three-dimensional, complex characters. What they have sold out, or turned around, are certain rules and conventions, in their pursuit of the new, the different, and the previously un- or under-represented, while remaining within the boundaries of a recognisable framework of practice. The question I sought to answer in this essay by a focus on character roles and characterisation strategies – how do crime writers create custom fit texts in an off-the-rack genre world? – goes to the heart of the nature of crime fiction as an evolutionary genre, a genre that has survived and developed because its practitioners have responded to social, political, economic, and cultural changes, and investigated these changes in their works. Proximal investigators, corpses of convenience, and families of circumstance come in multifarious forms, and I offer these three terms as a means by which we can consider some of the ways in which authors have risen to the challenge of both fulfilling and expanding readers', and their own, horizons of expectation.

Works Cited

Adler, Freda. Sisters in Crime: The Rise of the New Female Criminal. New York: McGraw-Hill, 1975.

Amis, Martin. *Night Train.* London: Vintage, 1997.

Atwood, Margaret. "Descent: Negotiating with the Dead." *Negotiating with the Dead: A Writer on Writing.* London: Virago, 2003. 137-61.

Benjamin, Walter. Charles Baudelaire: A Lyric Poet in the Era of High Capitalism. Trans. Harry Zohn. London: Verso, 1997.

Bentley, E. C. *Trent's Last Case.* London: Nelson, 1913.

"Best-Selling Fiction Author." *Guinness World Records* 2006. 25 Aug. 2006.
<http://www.guinnessworldrecords.com/content_pages/record.asp?recordid=48281>

Binyon, J. J. Murder Will Out: The Detective in Fiction. Oxford: Oxford UP, 1990.

Brand, Dana. "Reconstructing the 'Flaneur': Poe's Invention of the Detective Story." *Genre* 18.1 (1985): 36-56.

Brooks, Peter. *Reading for the Plot.* Oxford: Clarendon, 1984.

Campbell, Joseph. *The Hero with a Thousand Faces.* London: Fontana, 1993.

Cawelti, John G. *Adventure, Mystery, and Romance: Formula Stories As Art and Popular Culture.* Chicago: U of Chicago P, 1976.

Chandler, David. "An Introduction to Genre Theory." 5 July 2000. 25 July 2003. <http://www.aber.ac.uk/media/Documents/intgenre/intgenre.html>

Chandler, Raymond. *The Big Sleep*. Harmondsworth: Penguin, 1978.

---. The Notebooks of Raymond Chandler and English Summer: A Gothic Romance. Ed. Frank MacShane. New York: Ecco, 1976.

---. "The Simple Art of Murder." Haycraft, *The Art* 222-37.

Christie, Agatha. *Curtain: Poirot's Last Case*. Glasgow: Fontana, 1980.

---. *The Murder at the Vicarage*. Glasgow: Fontana, 1967.

---. *The Murder of Roger Ackroyd*. Glasgow: Fontana, 1957.

---. *Ordeal by Innocence*. Glasgow: Fontana, 1984.

---. *The Secret of Chimneys*. London: Pan, 1975.

Coben, Harlan. *Just One Look*. London: Orion, 2004.

Colie, Rosalie. *The Resources of Kind: Genre-Theory in the Renaissance*. Berkeley: U of California P, 1973.

Collins, Max Allan. *The History of Mystery*. Portland: Collectors, 2001.

Collins, Wilkie. *The Moonstone*. Oxford: Clio, 1992.

Cornwell, Patricia. *Point of Origin*. London: Little, Brown, 1998.

---. *Post-Mortem*. London: Warner, 1992.

---. *Unnatural Exposure*. London: Little, Brown, 1997.

Corris, Peter. *The Coast Road*. Crows Nest: Allen and Unwin, 2004.

Craig, Patricia, and Mary Cadogan. *The Lady Investigates: Women Detectives and Spies in Fiction*. London: Gollancz, 1981.

Crais, Robert. *The Forgotten* Man. London: Orion, 2006.

---. *L.A. Requiem*. London: Orion, 1999.

Danielsson, Karin Molander. "The Dynamic Detective: Special Interest and Seriality in

Contemporary Detective Series." Diss. Uppsala U, 2002.

Deaver, Jeffery. *The Empty Chair*. London: Coronet, 2000.

DeLillo, Don. *White Noise*. London: Picador, 1999.

DellaCava, Frances A., and Madeline H. Engel. *Sleuths in Skirts: Analysis and Bibliography of Serialized Female Sleuths*. New York: Routledge, 2002.

Dellamater, Jerome H., and Ruth Prigozy, eds. *Theory and Practice of Classic Detective Fiction*. Westport: Greenwood, 1997.

Didion, Joan. *Slouching towards Bethlehem*. New York: Washington Square, 1981.

Doyle, Arthur Conan. *Memories and Adventures*. London: Hodder, 1924.

Dubrow, Heather. *Genre*. London: Methuen, 1982.

Duff, David. Introduction. *Modern* 1-24.

---. "Key Concepts." *Modern* x-xvi.

---, ed. *Modern Genre Theory*. Harlow: Pearson Education, 2000.

Duras, Marguerite. *Practicalities: Marguerite Duras Speaks to Jerome Beaujour*. Trans. Barbara Bray. New York: Grove Weidenfeld, 1990.

Evanovich, Janet. *Ten Big Ones*. London: Headline, 2004.

"Family First Founder, Andrew Evans." *Religion Report*. ABC. Radio National, Brisbane. 29 Sept. 2004.

"Family First Refuses Preference Swap with Lesbians." *Age* 5 Oct. 2004. 18 Nov. 2004.
    <http://www.theage.com.au/articles/2004/10/05/1096871859778.html>

"Family First Senator Flags Abortion Debate." *Sydney Morning Herald* 3 Nov. 2004. 3 Nov. 2004.
    <http://www.smh.com.au/news/National/Family-First-senator-flags-abortion-debate/2000...>

Farrar, Stacy. "Democrats Do Deal with God." *Sydney Star Observer* 23 Sep. 2004. 18 Nov. 2004.
    <http://www.ssonet.com.au/archives/display.asp?articleID=4376>

Fishelov, David. *Metaphors of Genre: The Role of Analogies in Genre Theory*. Pennsylvania: Pennsylvania State UP, 1993.

Fowler, Alastair. Kinds of Literature: An Introduction to the Theory of Genres and Modes. Oxford: Clarendon, 1982.

Gabbard, Glen O. The Psychology of the Sopranos. New York: Basic, 2002.

Gelder, Ken. Popular Fiction: The Logics and Practices of a Literary Field. London: Routledge, 2004.

Goddard, Robert. Dying to Tell. London: Corgi, 2002.

Godwin, William. The Adventures of Caleb Williams, or, Things as They Are. Ed. Herbert Van Thal. London: Cassell, 1966.

Grafton, Sue. Q Is for Quarry. London: Macmillan, 2002.

---. R Is for Ricochet. New York: Pan, 2004.

---. S Is for Silence. New York: Macmillan, 2005.

Greene, Richard, and Peter Vernezze, eds. The Sopranos and Philosophy: I Kill Therefore I Am. Chicago: Open Court, 2004.

Gregory, Sinda. Private Investigations: The Novels of Dashiell Hammett. Carbondale: Southern Illinois UP, 1985.

Hammett, Dashiell. The Maltese Falcon. Harmondsworth: Penguin, 1963.

Hansen, Joseph. Nightwork: A Dave Brandstetter Mystery. London: Owen, 1984.

Haycraft, Howard, ed. The Art of the Mystery Story. New York: Grosset and Dunlap, 1947.

Healy, Patrick. "8 Years Later, a Flight 800 Memorial for Some Friends." Associated Retired Aviation Professionals. 17 July 2004. 2 July 2006.

<http://www.twa800.com/news/nyt-7-17-04.htm>

Highsmith, Patricia. *Ripley's Game*. New York: Knopf, 1974.

---. *The Talented Mr Ripley*. London: Heinemann, 1966.

Høeg, Peter. *Miss Smilla's Feeling for Snow*. Trans. F. David. London: Flamingo, 1994.

"An Interview with Sara." *Sara Paretsky*. Undated. 28 Aug. 2006. <http://www.saraparetsky.com/sarainterview.html>

Jackson, Christine A. *Myth and Ritual in Women's Detective Fiction*. Jefferson: McFarland, 2002.

Jauss, Hans Robert. *Toward an Aesthetic of Reception*. Trans. Timothy Bahti. Brighton: Harvester, 1982.

Jung, Carl Gustav. *The Archetypes and the Collective Unconscious*. 2nd ed. Trans. R. F. C. Hull. Princeton: Princeton UP, 1969.

Kemelman, Harry. *Thursday the Rabbi Walked Out*. London: Hutchinson, 1979.

Klein, Kathleen Gregory, ed. *Women Times Three: Writers, Detectives, Readers*. Bowling Green: Bowling Green State U Popular P, 1995.

Knight, Stephen. *Crime Fiction, 1800-2000*. Basingstoke: Palgrave Macmillan, 2004.

Knox, Ronald. "Detective Story Decalogue." Haycraft. *The Art* 194-96.

Kundera, Milan. *The Art of the Novel*. Trans. Linda Asher. London: Faber, 1988.

Leonard, Elmore. "Easy on the Hooptedoodle: 10 Rules for Writing." *Mystery Ink: The Booklover's Guide to Mysteries and Thrillers*. Undated. 9 Oct. 2004. <http://www.mysteryinkonline.com/writingrules.htm>

Lynch, Deidre Shauna. *The Economy of Character: Novels, Market Culture and the Business of Inner Meaning*. Chicago: U of Chicago P, 1998.

Malmgren, Carl. *Anatomy of Murder: Mystery, Detective, and Crime Fiction*. Ohio: Bowling Green State U Popular P, 2001.

Mankell, Henning. *Faceless Killers*. Trans. Steven T. Murray. London: Harvill, 2000.

---. *A Touch of Frost*. Trans. Ebba Segerberg. London: Vintage, 2005.

Marriage Amendment Act of 2004. No. 126. Canberra: Australian Government, 2004.

Messent, Peter, ed. "Introduction: From Private Eye to Police Procedural – The Logic of Contemporary Crime Fiction." *Criminal Proceedings: The Contemporary American Crime Novel*. Chicago: Pluto, 1997. 1-21.

Mosley, Walter. *Devil in a Blue Dress*. London: Serpent's Tail, 1991.

Munich. Dir. Steven Spielberg. Universal, 2005.

The New Shorter Oxford English Dictionary on Historical Principles. Ed. Lesley Brown. 2 vols. Oxford: Oxford UP, 1993.

Oates, Joyce Carol. "The Simple Art of Murder." *New York Review of Books* 21 Dec. 1995: 32-40.

Paretsky, Sara. *Bitter Medicine*. Harmondsworth: Penguin, 1987.

---. *Blacklist*. London: Hamish Hamilton, 2003.

---. *Burn Marks*. London: Virago, 1991.

---. *Deadlock*. Harmondsworth: Penguin, 1987.

---. *Fire Sale*. London: Hodder, 2005.

---. *Guardian Angel*. Harmondsworth: Penguin, 1992.

---. *Hard Time*. London: Hamish Hamilton, 1999.

---. *Indemnity Only*. Harmondsworth: Penguin, 1987.

---. *Killing Orders*. Harmondsworth: Penguin, 1987.

---. "Literary Dissent." *Refuse and Resist*. Undated. 28 Dec. 2006.

<http://www.refuseandresist.org/article-print.php?aid=1167>

---. *Total Recall*. London: Penguin, 2002.

---. *Toxic Shock*. Harmondsworth: Penguin, 1990.

---. "Truth, Lies and Duct Tape." *Sara Paretsky*. Undated. 28 August
2006.
<http://www.saraparetsky.com/silence.html>

---. *V. I. for Short*. London: Hamish Hamilton, 1995.

---. "Writing a Series Character." *Writing Mysteries: A Handbook by
the Mystery Writers of America*. Ed. Sue Grafton. Cincinnati: Writer's Digest Books, 1992. 55-60.

Pelecanos, George. *A Firing Offence*. New York: Serpent's Tail, 1997.

Plain, Gill. *Twentieth Century Crime Fiction: Gender, Sexuality and the Body*. Edinburgh: Edinburgh UP, 2001.

Poe, Edgar Allan. *The Complete Tales of Mystery and Imagination; The Raven and Other Poems*. London: Octopus, 1981.

---. "The Man of the Crowd." Poe, *The Complete* 164-69.

---. "The Murders in the Rue Morgue." Poe, *The Complete* 59-80.

"The Poetry of David Malouf." *Poetica*. ABC. Radio National, Brisbane. 20 Mar. 2004.

Porter, Dennis. *The Pursuit of Crime: Art and Ideology in Detective Fiction*. New Haven: Yale UP, 1981.

Porter, Dorothy. *The Monkey's Mask*. Melbourne: Hyland, 1994.

Priestman, Martin. *Detective Fiction and Literature: The Figure on the Carpet*. New York: St Martin's, 1991.

Propp, Vladimir. *Morphology of the Folktale*. Trans. Laurence Scott. Austin: U of Texas P, 1968.

Puzo, Mario. *The Godfather*. London: Pan, 1970.

Reddy, Maureen T. "The Feminist Counter-Tradition in Crime: Cross, Grafton, Paretsky, and Wilson." *Cunning Craft: Original Essays on Detective Fiction and Literary Theory*. Eds. R. G. Walker and J. M. Frazer. Macomb: Western Illinois P, 1990. 174-87.

Rennison, Nick, ed. *Bloomsbury Good Reading Guide to Crime Fiction*. London: Bloomsbury, 2003.

Reynolds, Moira Davidson. *Women Authors of Detective Series: Twenty-One American and British Writers, 1900-2000.* Jefferson: McFarland, 2001.

Sayers, Dorothy L. "The Omnibus of Crime." *Detective Fiction: A Collection of Critical Essays.* Ed. Robin W. Winks. Englewood Cliffs: Prentice-Hall, 1980. 53-83.

Shakespeare, William. "The Tragedy of Macbeth." *The Complete Oxford Shakespeare: Volume III – Tragedies.* 3 vols. Eds. Stanley Wells, et al. Oxford: Oxford UP, 1987. 1307-34.

The Social Work Dictionary. Robert Barker. Silver Spring: National Association of Social Workers, 1988.

The Sopranos: The Complete First Season. DVD. HBO Home Video, 1999.

The Sopranos: The Complete Second Season. DVD. HBO Home Video, 2000.

Stevenson, Robert Louis. *The Strange Case of Dr. Jekyll and Mr. Hyde, and Other Stories.* Ed. Jenni Calder. New York: Penguin, 1979. 27-97.

Stoker, Bram. *Dracula.* Ed. Maurice Hindle. London: Penguin, 1993.

Symons, Julian. *Bloody Murder: From the Detective Story to the Crime Novel: A History.* London: Faber, 1972.

Taylor, Andrew. "The Strange Appeal of Crime Fiction." *Shots: The Magazine for Crime and Mystery.* Undated. 22 Aug.2004. <http://www.shotsmag.co.uk/ANDREW%TAYLOR%20CRIME. htm>

Tennyson, Alfred. "Sir Galahad." *Tennyson.* Plain Texts of the Poets. St Lucia: U of Queensland P, 1968. 48-50.

Tester, Keith, ed. *The Flaneur.* London: Routledge, 1994.

Todorov, Tzvetan. *The Fantastic: A Structual Approach to a Literary Genre.* Trans. Richard Howard. Cleveland: Case Western Reserve UP, 1973.

---. *Introduction to Poetics.* Trans. Richard Howard. Brighton: Harvester, 1981.

---. *Mikhail Bakhtin: The Dialogical Principle.* Trans. Wlad Godzich. Theory and History of Literature. Minneapolis: U of Minnesota P, 1984.

---. "Structural Analysis of Narrative." *Novel* 3.1(1969): 70-76.

---. "The Typology of Detective Fiction." *The Poetics of Prose.* Trans. Richard Howard. Oxford: Blackwell, 1977. 42-52.

Thomson, Ian. "The Wallander Mystery." *Sydney Morning Herald* 3 Jan. 2004. 23 Aug. 2006.
<http://www.smh.com.au/articles/2004/01/02/1072908895024.html>

Toye, Randall. *The Agatha Christie Who's Who.* Aylesbury: Heron, 1980.

Tynyanov, Yury. "The Literary Fact." Duff, *Modern* 29-49.

Van Dine, S. S. "Twenty Rules for Writing Detective Stories." Haycraft, *The Art* 189-93.

Vogler, Christopher. *The Writer's Journey: Mythic Structure for Storytellers and Screenwriters.* London: Pan, 1996.

Walton, Priscilla L., and Manina Jones. *Detective Agency: Women Rewriting the Hard-Boiled Tradition.* Berkeley: U of California P, 1999.

Walters, Minette. *Acid Row.* Sydney: Allen and Unwin, 2001.

---. *The Shape of Snakes.* Sydney: Allen and Unwin, 2000.

"Who We Are." *Family First Party.* Undated. 30 Sep. 2004. <http://www.familyfirst.org.au/who/php>

Wilson, Barbara. *Murder in the Collective.* London: Women's, 1984.

Wright, Willard Huntington. "The Great Detective Stories." Haycraft, *The Art* 33-70.

Yacowar, Maurice. *The Sopranos on the Couch: Analyzing Television's Greatest Series.* New York: Continuum, 2003.

About the Author

Jay Verney is an Australian author who has published novels, essays, short stories, poetry, memoir, magazine and newspaper columns, book and film reviews, and comics.

Jay's first novel, ***A Mortality Tale***, was shortlisted for the Australian/*Vogel* and Miles Franklin Literary Awards (and is available as both a paperback and an ebook). Jay has a PhD (in genre and crime fiction), and a Master's degree (memoir) in Creative Writing from the University of Queensland. In 2009, she received a Dean's Award for Outstanding Research Higher Degree Thesis for her PhD. The book you're reading, and the novel, ***Summon Up The Blood*** (titled "Thicker Than Water" originally) are the two parts of that doctorate.

Jay's second novel, ***Percussion***, is now available in both ebook and paperback, as is her third novel, ***Spawned Secrets***. Her memoir, ***The Women Come and Go***, along with its companion essay, ***The Women Came and Went***, are available in one volume in both paperback and ebook formats. They're all sailing around on the mighty Amazon ready to accompany you home to your happy harbour.

Visit virtual Jay at her websites for **free** entertainment:

Transient Total Focus – www.jayverney.net

One blink at a time

Minty fresh stuff and nonsense and even some useful things.

Veranda Life – www.verandalife.com

Breathe ~ Relax ~ Drink Black Tea Often

999 lovely haikus with lovely images.

Zen Kettle – www.zenkettle.wordpress.com

It makes tea

Zenkus, teeny tiny haikus about life, the universe, and everything. Also lovely.

Last Cat On Mars – www.lastcatonmars.wordpress.com

Would you want to be the first?

Dr On Mars welcomes you to a comical world of fun and laughs. It's laughly, and lovely, yes.

You can give Jay all your money by visiting Amazon to purchase even more of her lovely works. Ask Prof. Google for 'Jay Verney Amazon.' You know you want to, grasshopper.

If you enjoyed this book, please don't hesitate to **visit Amazon and post a review**. The author will be so grateful, she'll send you a picture of your very own avatar in minifigure world posing with the martially famous Last Cat On Mars and also, a bonus ice-cream and naturally the blessings of her mother's violin bow.

Acknowledgements

I remain very grateful for the Australian Postgraduate Award that enabled me to undertake this research. It came at a most fortuitous time in our lives.

Thanks also to the staff at EMSAH at Qld Uni, particularly Angela Tuohy, Cathy Squirrell, and Vicky McNicol, for their support and good humour during my candidature.

I remain admiring of, indebted to, and inspired by three noteworthy divas, each of whom, in her own unique way, has made the world a much happier place to live in, especially for me:

- Bette Midler, the Divine Miss M – a transcendent concert on April 8, 2005, after a 25 year wait, and for once, the wait was worth it – Kiss My Brass, indeed.
- Makybe Diva – 3 minutes, 19.79 seconds, carrying 58 kgs to her third Melbourne Cup win in November 2005 – proving yet again my father, Jim's motto: nothing can beat a great stayer, not to mention the mystical value of the number three: the whole set, Maisie, just for you.
- Finally, most importantly, Lorrie Lawler – take it as read.